D0882612

PLANTING
AND REAPING
ALBRIGHT

Burke O. Long

PLANTING AND REAPING ALBRIGHT

Politics, Ideology, and Interpreting the Bible

The Pennsylvania State University Press
University Park, Pennsylvania

Library of Congress Cataloging-in-Publication Data

Long, Burke O.
  Planting and reaping Albright : politics, ideology, and interpreting the Bible /
Burke O. Long.
        p.   cm.
  Includes bibliographical references and index.
  ISBN 0-271-01576-4 (alk. paper)
  1. Albright, William Foxwell, 1891–1971.   2. Bible scholars—United States—
Biography.   3. Bible—Criticism, interpretation, etc.—History—20th century.
I. Title.
BS501.A43L66   1997
220'.092—dc20
  [B]   95-42065
                                                                                          CIP

It is the policy of The Pennsylvania University Press to use acid-free paper for
the first printing of all clothbound books. Publications on uncoated stock satisfy
the minimum requirements of American National Standard for Information
Sciences—Permanence of Paper for Printed Library Materials, ANSI Z39.48-1992.

For my family—Judith, Melissa, Timothy

Contents

Acknowledgments

I acknowledge with pleasure a few people and institutions whose support for my work has been both generous and critical to whatever success it may be accorded. The American Philosophical Society in Philadelphia awarded me a research grant during 1991–92; without this stipend and the friendly, professional assistance from the Society's librarians, I would not have been able to consult Albright's papers. Bowdoin College aided my work with a number of research grants. David Noel Freedman spent valuable time answering my questions, read early drafts of material, and most importantly, made certain of his personal files available to this outsider's scrutiny. Edward F. Campbell, Jr., provided information on the Biblical Colloquium, and Mrs. G. Ernest (Emily) Wright graciously responded to my queries about her husband's activities related to the Colloquium. Charles Bright kindly provided copies of letters written by his father, John Bright, to others of the Albright school. John J. Collins offered me an epistolary occasion to clarify my thinking, and I am grateful that he was then willing to become a character in my narratives. I am indebted to a number of other scholars, all of whom were trained at Harvard's graduate program in Near Eastern Languages and Civilizations, for sharing their views on the legacy of Albright in Cambridge, Massachusetts. One of their number, S. Dean McBride, offered forceful and helpful criticism of an earlier draft of this material. I followed some of his advice, and I trust he will understand the theoretical reasons why in some cases I did not.

Finally, I thank Carol Schneidewind for her untiring assistance in working with many revisions of these essays. Even in an age of personal computers, such a skilled typist and proofreader has not become obsolete.

Portions of Chapters 3 and 4, although now substantially rewritten, were published in earlier forms: "Mythic Trope in the Autobiography of William Foxwell Albright," *Biblical Archaeologist* 56:1 (1993): 36–45; "W. F. Albright, G. E. Wright, and the Legacies of Christian Hebraism," *Proceedings of the Eleventh World Congress of Jewish Studies, Division A* (Jerusalem: World Union of Jewish Studies, 1994), 239–46. I am grateful to the publishers for permission to draw on these original exploratory ventures into the Albrightean world.

1 LETTERS AND FRAME-SHOTS
A Perspective on Albright

"It is an engrossing article," John Collins, editor of the *Journal of Biblical Literature* wrote to me in midsummer 1993. "And I do not doubt its interest to our readers." Collins referred to an essay about a four-volume theological dictionary planned by George Ernest Wright and William Foxwell Albright during the 1940s. The dictionary was not completed, and my article about it was rejected for publication.

Collins continued, "As you intimated, however, it is not the sort of thing we usually publish (it really has to do with the politics of scholarship rather than even the history of scholarship)." Both of his manuscript readers, Collins wrote, advised against publication, "strictly on the grounds of genre."[1]

Although a rejected article is not an unusual event in academic publishing, this episode stimulated a series of letters between us which, I realized later, helped me explain the grounds of inquiry of the book you are about to read. This study of William Foxwell Albright and the "Baltimore school" is about *both* the history and politics of scholarship, and about their inseparability. It has to do with complex bundles of commitments, some explicit, many implicit, which these scholars built into their practice of a highly technical craft. I have sought to recover traces of such commitments encoded in the texts—letters, notes, diaries, official minutes, published scholarship—that document the construction of knowledge. I have construed the Albrighteans'

1. John J. Collins to Burke O. Long, July 13, 1993.

production of knowledge about the Bible through a postmodern lens. I view it not as innocently objective learning, conforming to the master paradigm of scientific rationality, but as aggregates of interested actions that sustained various personal and institutional relations. I speak of episodes in the history of biblical scholarship, but in ways that explore social and political dynamics at work when members of the Albright, or Baltimore, "school" researched, constructed, and disseminated their claims to knowledge.

Given this general perspective, the essays in this book offer glimpses into a culture of like-minded scholars who constructed and mediated knowledge through ideologically charged social processes. In the first study (Chapter 2), I interpret a small society of scholars, the Biblical Colloquium, as a powerful social mechanism through which a few students of Albright planted, nurtured, and harvested elements of their teacher's approach to biblical study. In its first decade the Colloquium was remarkable for its collective ambition and will to dominate American biblical scholarship. Members wanted to assure, as one participant put it, that the future would belong to Albright's school of thought.

In a second essay (Chapter 3), I examine plans that Albright and others made during the 1940s for a dictionary of biblical languages. I read events in terms of conflicting ideologies held by Christian and Jew, scientist and theologian, and their admixture in Albrightean biblical scholarship of the time. Though obscured by codes of scientific scholarship, such suppressed disturbances surfaced as claims to privileged power and normative status for Albrightean biblical studies, backed by an aggressive denominational publishing program, met with resistive action.

Finally, in a third essay (Chapter 4), I consider a metaphor Albright used to characterize himself as emergent biblical scientist. As a recent graduate of Johns Hopkins, and under the press of archaeological fact discovered in British Mandate Palestine, he later recalled, the young Albright passed from skepticism about the Bible to conviction about its historical trustworthiness. Study of this arresting figure of speech allows me to explore Albright's embrace of scientist as cultural hero and the mythification of Self as Master Knower. I then consider the power of such an artifact of self to shape the disciplinary language of biblical archaeology, a field of learning that, perhaps more than any other, carries the legacy of Albright's formidable contributions.

Although Albright is a main character in my narratives, each of these essays involves certain of his students as well. Members of the "Baltimore school" saw themselves as sons and grandsons of Albright, and because they built such patriarchal concepts into their social and academic practice they constituted a sociological phenomenon that had lasting consequences for American intellectual history and scholarship. In this general sense, then, this book will suggest ways in which Albright, or rather a social realization of Albright, was present in, and presented to, a culture of generational and ideological solidarity.

Given the perspective that governs my study of the Albrighteans, it will surprise no one that I believe the distinction John Collins made between *history* of scholarship and *politics* of scholarship involves more than, as he later would write, merely an ad hoc reference to the suitability of my essay for the *Journal*. Now, through conjury of imagination, and reading those letters again, two friendly debaters emerge from the written pages. Re-creating words of many others who contribute to the culture of critically oriented biblical studies, Collins and Long also manage to find their own voices to state difference and agreement.[2]

> BOL: I've given up the conviction of being able to speak out of a position of objectivity that appeals to some non-contingent ground as the basis for my claims to say something true. Speech constructs selves, and our selves' worlds of meaning. Speech is thus rooted in social relationships involving power (politics), ideologies (representations of "how things are") and values (shifting, situational configurations of preferred "goods"). Thus, the distinction between the "politics of scholarship" and the "history of scholarship," given my premise, is incoherent. For the history of scholarship (the practice of scholars in the past) and the *writing* of that history (a reading of that practice) are both politically and ideologically charged activities. I cannot speak from on high about what constitutes scholarship, but I can critique from various standpoints the practices of scholars, and seek to lay bare some of the problematic presuppositions which informed their work, and the ambiguous situations, filled with positive resolves and conflicted hesitations, in which they lived out their lives. And I invite others to do the same for me, not from a position of universal normativeness, but from a position of contested difference that seeks constant critical reflection on the foundational assumptions of scholarly work.

2. These slightly edited excerpts are drawn from letters written in August and September 1993.

JCC: The distinction I made between the "politics of scholarship" and "the history of scholarship" was an ad hoc distinction with reference to suitability for *JBL* [*Journal of Biblical Literature*]. An article dealing with Wright's views on the conquest belongs to the history of scholarship, even if it deals with the underlying theological/political/ideological prejudices, in a way that his correspondence with the press [planning to publish the dictionary] does not. It is very unusual for *JBL* to publish an article that does not focus on the interpretation of a text. I did not mean to suggest that scholarship is not political (in the very broad sense in which you use the word).

I think it is a little disingenuous of you, however, to say that you have given up any claim of objectivity. I would not have guessed that from your article. (You did not respond to my query about [your vantage point of implied pure objectivity when you said that in planning for the theological dictionary] the Hebrew Bible [was] being read *against itself* as a Christian text. . . . And if you are not speaking from "on high," it would be interesting to know from where you are speaking.

Actually, I don't think the methodological and theoretical differences between us are very significant (and I'm not yet clear on the ideological ones). Few people nowadays claim complete objectivity, but most of us entertain it as an ideal, in the sense that we try to rein in our prejudices and take account of other points of view. I assume that you aspire to an *accurate* account of Albright, and if you do, this presupposes some kind of an ideal of objectivity. (If accuracy is not a relevant ideal, then we may have some serious misunderstanding between us.)

BOL: I did not write that I had "given up any claim of objectivity." That sounds much more absolutist than I wish to be, and rests on a conceptual polarity that I do not share. I mean the opposition of objective to subjective: that which is eternal, public, knowable to reason in the classic philosophical sense of "essence" set over against the subjective—private, idiosyncratic, contingent, in the classic sense of "accident." I wrote a contextualized, or "deconstructed," form of that polarity. I've given up claiming to speak "out of a position of objectivity *that appeals to some non-contingent ground*" [emphasis added] for its truth, that is, from some point (such as eternal reason) that is presumed to be removed from the social interactions, including linguistic transactions, that make up our human circumstances.

"Objectivity," then, has not disingenuously disappeared from my vocabulary; the word simply points to a status I give to statements about the world, a status that is variable, rooted in the social processes of creating knowledge and social consensus about what is known.

"Objectivity" is therefore considerably less grand than the classical philosophers or popular usage might suppose, but not identical at all with [what is] private and individualistic. I believe that "objectivity" takes its meaning within a body of discourse shared by a group of people who construct their sense of how things are in the world—with variations, certainly, but also with a good number of assumptions held in common. Accordingly, the notion of "object" logically has to be freed of its usual associations with essentialist philosophy and reconceived. Whatever comes at me in the world (that is, an "object"), I construct through language. So the "hardness" of object, its common-sense separateness from observer, is mitigated by this involvement of speaker-subject-creator, who has a say not only in constructing how an object appears and what it means, but also in creating a sense of its separateness from subject-observer. The commonsense dichotomy between subject and object breaks down, and with it the epistemology that undergirds it. "Truth," then, becomes perspectival, a hermeneutical construction, a matter of relationality—how I stand in relation to what is given to me. I don't believe statements can be evaluated for their "objectivity" from a point outside this social matrix, but they may be evaluated for cogency according to the rules of the discourse being employed. Or they may be evaluated as to the effects of *holding* certain things to be true.

Within this circumscribed social reality, I think it fair to say that I "try to rein in our [my] prejudices and take account of other points of view." One way of doing this is to be self-aware of the theoretical grounds of discourse (whether it be rooted in the disciplines of history, literary theory, linguistics, social or natural science, etc.), so as to discard those *other* kinds of discourse-based, or discipline-specific prejudices that do not cohere with the particular mode of inquiry.

As to "accuracy," the question you raise, I doubt if there is a point of reference outside of these defined social settings of speech by which to judge "accuracy." I'm coming to think that "accuracy," like "meaning," is situational and relational, and meaningful in limited circumstances, and subject to all the problematical and particular circumstances of speech and interpretation. The "facts," say of the past, are there for all to see in a way, but we see differently and relationally. Who can disentangle such constructed "facts" from interpretive constructs, except perhaps from the most trivial of the facts?

What I'm struggling to figure out is how to write myself into the language of historiography, which by habit and custom is tied to a model of "objectivity" that no longer works for me. You are right that my article "sounds" as though I claim some noncontingent objectivity. Its tone and implied subject position seem conventionally "objective." Or to put it another way: conventional language of historiography implies a persona, the self as knower of objectivities, that obscures my chosen subject position: the relationality of how I, as linguistically formed subject, construct knowledge out of what is given from the "past." I've thought of writing myself into an introductory chapter so as to provide a framework for reading the typically "objectivist" prose of the individual studies that will follow. But I'm not very happy with only that as a solution because it does not address adequately the power of conventional language to suggest what I do not wish it to suggest (and what if people skip the introduction?).

By the way, your query about the Bible being read *against* itself as a Christian text is an apt example of the trouble I'm having. [I originally suggested that since the publishers insisted that a Christian theologian be listed as the main author/editor of the Hebrew dictionary, disregarding the Jewish scholar who would do most of the philological work, then, in effect "the Hebrew Bible was to be read against itself, that is, *not* as an ancient document, but as a *Christian* text."] Here's a new formulation of the sentence: "Acceding to the editor's demand, however, meant that the Hebrew Bible would be read not as an *ancient* document, as presumed by the ideologies of scientific investigation, but as a *Christian* text, thus subverting one set of ideological principles by adherence to another."

JCC: I have one mischievous question: Does the theory make much difference to how we proceed in practice? Do we not in any case try to account for the evidence and formulate hypotheses as to intentions, motives, etc.? Is the difference largely a matter of the degree of confidence we have in our hypotheses (or our awareness of their hypothetical nature)?

It was a fair and perceptive question, not simply mischievous. It lingers, and will demand its response as the conjury fades. As may be surmised, I locate this study, and more to the point, myself, somewhere on the shifting borders between modernism, that cultural river of belief in the objectivities of scientific reason, and the array of resistance to its flooding dominance called, for better or worse, postmodernism.[3] I assume, with Nietzsche, that human situations, like the powerful presence of scientific rationality, are products of human history, though many people may be convinced that at least some notions or ways of behaving in the world directly mirror mandates and patterns of timeless reality. Such convictions about the naturalness and permanence of certain aspects of human experience discourage anyone from treating particular views, habits, institutions, and values as contingent creations arising at a definite time and, with different decisions, ceasing to exist.

With loss of confidence in an unassailable objective ground for truth has come a turn away from master narratives and dominating perspectives that imply mastery of a world of objects by a fully cognizant and autonomous knower. This shift has encouraged a focus on the plurality of linguistic, socially grounded processes through which human beings construct their truths and their maps of reality from within their limited psychosocial contexts. Postmodern thinkers have swerved from object-out-there toward reader, whether it be the reader of a literary text, a social phenomenon, or the physicalities of what is ordered by our constructions of natural processes.[4] Jacques Derrida has complicated even this swerve toward reader by arguing that text-out-there and reader, and their difference from each other (the sharp distinction between knowing subject and known object), are all constructs of

---

3. See Ihab Hassan, *The Postmodern Turn: Essays in Postmodern Theory and Culture* (Columbus: Ohio State University Press, 1987); Madan Sarup, *An Introductory Guide to Post-Structuralism and Postmodernism*, 2d ed. (Athens: University of Georgia Press, 1993); Linda Hutcheon, *A Poetics of Postmodernism: History, Theory, Fiction* (New York: Routledge & Kegan Paul, 1988); idem, *The Politics of Postmodernism* (New York: Routledge & Kegan Paul, 1989); David Harvey, *The Condition of Postmodernity* (Oxford: Basil Blackwell, 1989). For applications to biblical studies, see above all Gary Phillips, ed., "Poststructural Criticism and the Bible: Text/History/Discourse," *Semeia* 51 (1990); George Aichele/The Bible Collective, *The Postmodern Bible* (New Haven: Yale University Press, 1995); A. K. M. Adam, *What Is Postmodern Biblical Criticism?* (Minneapolis: Augsburg Fortress, 1995); Stephen Moore, *Post-structuralism and the New Testament: Derrida and Foucault at the Foot of the Cross* (Minneapolis: Augsburg Fortress, 1994). For a view that postmodernism may be running its course, see Gregory Bruce, "Cracks in the Walls of the Postmodern Monastery: Bibliographic Leak or Ruin?" *Critical Review of Books in Religion* 5 (1992): 1–38 (with full bibliography); also Christopher Norris, *What's Wrong with Postmodernism: Critical Theory and the Ends of Philosophy* (Baltimore: Johns Hopkins University Press, 1990).

4. See Richard Rorty, *Philosophy and the Mirror of Nature* (Oxford: Blackwell, 1980); *Objectivity, Relativism, and Truth* (New York: Cambridge University Press, 1991).

language. One's conscious relation to the "is-ness" of the world, therefore, is not seen as positive, direct, unmediated knowledge, but as interpretive construct. Both the "world-as-it-is" and the observing, reflecting self, or "subject," are constituted as intelligible and significant, as "real," through constructs of language rooted in the conditions of material and social life.

To the extent that I locate myself in this landscape, I do not guarantee the meanings I assert about Albright and his students with an appeal to some ground outside historically and institutionally situated, contingent speech. I construct meaning of what is given to me in the world. In the case of Albright, I detect ideologically charged events from a batch of letters which, when held up to the light, reveal trace lines of conceptual and personal associations, the stuff of conviction and intentionality, inscribed in scholarly discourse as well as friendly chitchat. I do not establish the meaning of such traces in any permanent or definitive way. Rather, I create narratives that encode the provisionalities of stating, with truthfulness, what my framing perspectives allow to be seen.

Representing "how things are" fixes meaning only temporarily, and in retrospect, or so Derrida claimed. With him, I view meaning, the creation of knowledge, as not only historical, but unstable. It is produced in complicated processes of focusing and framing, defining consensus, accepting agreed-upon contexts of meaningfulness. In turn, at least theoretically, all that may be dismantled; and by defining another context, or even by choosing entirely different foundational assumptions, that particular configuration of what the world gives us may be reconfigured.[5]

I do not present a master narrative about the Albrighteans in this book. I create instead a number of lesser narratives, frame-shots on scholarly activities that I have been able to construct out of various sources. I have researched my topics and written my narratives in the shadow of Foucault's theory on the perspectivity of knowledge and the interdependence of power and knowledge in constructing the social conditions under which we live.[6]

5. Jacques Derrida, *Of Grammatology*, trans. Gayatri Chakravorty Spivak (Baltimore: Johns Hopkins University Press, 1976); *Speech and Phenomena, and Other Essays on Husserl's Theory of Signs*, trans. David B. Allison (Evanston: Northwestern University Press, 1973); *Writing and Difference*, trans. Alan Bass (Chicago: University of Chicago Press, 1978).

6. Michel Foucault, *The Order of Things: An Archaeology of the Human Sciences* (New York: Pantheon, 1970); *The Archaeology of Knowledge*, trans. Alan Sheridan (New York: Pantheon, 1972); *Language, Counter-Memory, Practice: Selected Essays and Interviews*, ed. Donald Bouchard; trans. Donald Bouchard and Sherry Simon (Ithaca: Cornell University Press, 1977); *Power/Knowledge: Selected Interviews and Other Writings, 1972–1977*, ed. Colin Gordon; trans. Colin Gordon et al. (New York: Pantheon, 1980).

I have taken from Foucault the notion of "discourse," a linguistic practice such as scientific discourse or literary discourse which systematically forms the objects of which it speaks—for example, a subatomic "particle" that is discourse-formed in metaphors of solidity and mathematical equations; or a poem that is realized in the spaces between poet and reader through one of the several disciplined language-sets of literary criticism. From this perspective, I narrate episodes of Albrightean scholarly practice as struggles over meaning and discourse within a world of linguistic practice. My narratives are not about stable, objective realities that exist somehow independently of the language-frames that the Albrighteans used, or that I employ today.

I also look for ideology embedded in such linguistically realized conditions of the Albrighteans' scholarly lives. I think of ideology as a loose aggregate of commitments to values and assumptions about reality, "the way things really are." In this case, ideology has to do with what Albright and his students believed consensually, or better, *lived*, in their meaning-creating practices which sustained various social relations of domination or resistance.[7] In this sense, ideology is not so much a belief to which one may or may not subscribe, or a slogan for political revolutionaries, but rather more a bundle of *lived* commitments that are affirmed or challenged in concrete social interactions. I seek to make visible such allegiances imprinted on scholarly activities; I also note how ideology, often unnoticed, preserves or resists social formations, such as an academic institution, a "school" of scholars, a professional organization, a publishing house, a protocol of the acceptable for journal publication, or patrons of scholarly research.

Obviously, I do not write conventional biography, and I do not claim to have represented a life span of Albright's or his students' careers.[8] Nor is the history of biblical studies presented in the usual way. A reader will not find Albright plotted within an encompassing narrative of accumulating discoveries and assured knowledge. Such is common enough and offers one way of appreciating Albright's place in twentieth-century studies of the Bible.[9]

---

7. See Terry Eagleton, *Ideology: An Introduction* (New York: Verso, 1991); Jorge Larrain, *The Concept of Ideology* (Athens: University of Georgia Press, 1979); John Thompson, *Studies in the Theory of Ideology* (Berkeley and Los Angeles: University of California Press, 1984).

8. See Leona Glidden Running and David Noel Freedman, *William Foxwell Albright: A Twentieth-Century Genius* (New York: Morgan Press, 1975). Several tributes and memorial sketches may be found in David Noel Freedman, *The Published Works of William Foxwell Albright: A Comprehensive Bibliography* (Cambridge, Mass.: American Schools of Oriental Research, 1975), 3–40.

9. See, for example, P. R. S. Moorey, *A Century of Biblical Archaeology* (Cambridge: Lutterworth, 1991).

To make more visible what is often left unseen in such master narratives, I highlight assumed values and ideological commitments in relation to the exercise of social power. In short, I offer an alternative way to envision biblical criticism, its practitioners, and its history as academic enterprise.

I hope my argument will not be taken as an effort to reject out-of-hand the kind of rationalistic biblical criticism that Albright practiced. It would be foolish to impugn his or his students' innovative and fundamental contributions to the field at the time. Albright believed unreservedly in the methodologies of modernist science. He knew the limits of science but also was convinced of its possibilities for achieving objective knowledge about ancient history and civilizations, especially the "lands of the Bible." Within this framework he contributed as few others did to creating a twentieth-century American biblical archaeology that could stand before the bar of critical and scientific scholarship.

Of course, I do not share his conviction about the privileged normative-ness of such an approach. My dissent provides an opportunity to investigate constellations of ideological commitments, the vested interests of scientific scholarship that may be seen as linked to Albright's discovery, and syn-thesizing of new information gleaned from artifact and inscription. I offer narratives of contested claims to knowledge expressed through ideologically charged social and political processes, not a story of disembodied ideas.

I have tried to avoid premises rooted in some realm of eternal idea. I am trying not to treat the Albrighteans' object of study (the Bible), the methods of biblical study (historically oriented exegesis or explanation of the Bible), or the accumulated results of such studies (history, religion, theology of the Bible) as truths self-evidently grounded in objective and universally normative structures of scientific reason. By starting from a different mark, such as assuming the power of societal forces in human affairs, and by taking a limiting focus on the role of ideology and perspective in knowledge-making, I seek to understand something of the social and political grounding of the Albrighteans as they practiced their craft. Indirectly, I suggest the value of such a perspective for understanding the work of other scholars as well, including my own efforts.

The result is a radical historicizing of both scholars and the topics they study. On the one hand, Albright and his students, some of whom have become anecdotal exemplars of uncommon brilliance and great truths, are rendered in smaller, human terms, caught in the ambiguities of positive resolve and conflicted hesitation. On the other hand, the assumption that the field of biblical criticism is characterized by objectively grounded approaches to a unified object of study, namely the stable text of the Bible "out there," is rendered complex and problematic. In short, study of the Bible becomes more fully historical. What the Bible *is*, and what constitutes assured knowledge *about* the Bible, emerge in scholars' varied ideologically and politically charged encounters through which they configure "the Bible" and define bodies of knowledge.[10]

Such a perspective on the history of biblical studies is, of course, a peculiar construction of our own late twentieth-century age, when confidence in the ideals and political innocence of objectivist notions of scholarly knowledge has weakened. Mine is not a counsel of despair, however, but of hope. I suggest one way to conceive and write pieces of a history of knowledge-making among professional biblical critics, while owning up to the various contests of vested interest that make knowledge possible and inevitably open to challenge.

The private sources for these essays consist of Albright's voluminous correspondence with family, former students, and colleagues now available to the public for study at the Library of the American Philosophical Society in Philadelphia. In addition to approximately six thousand letters, the archive contains unpublished lectures, diaries, archaeological field notes, photographs, and other memorabilia relating to Albright's professional work. This treasure trove offers unusual opportunities to construct a more comprehensive picture of Albright's career than I have done and, incidentally, to dispute or corroborate my interpretations of the documents.

Working extensively with these archival sources, and considering them as part of the context for understanding Albright's more public activity, chiefly his published works, I reconstruct episodes that join together the private and public worlds of biblical scholarship as practiced first of all by Albright, and second, by former students who called themselves the "Albright gang" or, as Albright preferred, the "Baltimore school." I try to show how the Albrighteans worked with some success, at least for a time, to make their particular approach to the Bible the norm of biblical criticism in mid-century America.

Why have I chosen to focus on Albright? First, by many measures Albright was a forceful presence in biblical studies from the early to mid-twentieth

---

10. See Edward L. Greenstein, "The State of Biblical Studies; or, Biblical Studies in a State," in his *Essays on Biblical Method and Translation* (Brown Judaic Studies 92; Atlanta: Scholars Press, 1989), 3–27. By focusing on a few perennial disagreements in the history of biblical scholarship, Greenstein helps us glimpse the roles of foundational premise and theory, as well as theology and ideology, in practices of modern biblical critics.

century. Not only did he put a rather personal stamp on biblical archaeology as it developed through the American Schools of Oriental Research, but many of his students carried on in his tradition, leaving tangible traces of a sociological phenomenon in the culture of academic life.[11]

Long after Albright retired from active teaching, the legacy was strong at Harvard University, where George Ernest Wright and Frank Moore Cross, two of Albright's students from the 1930s and 1940s, trained successive generations, always with Albright as background mentor. One Harvard student from the 1970s recalled that the sense of kinship was explicit: "You were grandchildren of Albright. He [Frank Cross] is Albright's son. . . . I think we were told at some point that Albright was [his teacher Paul] Haupt's son." Another student from the 1980s evoked memories of a patriarchal shrine:

> Out in the alcove outside of Cross's office there were two framed black and white photographs on the wall, one of Ernest Wright and one of Albright, both in fairly—I won't say old age, I'd say advanced middle age. They weren't youthful pictures of them. They were side by side. I don't think there were plaques under them with the names. There was nothing else up on the wall. I remember it was a very dark color paint, maybe a deep green of some sort, and this was the room where the students all had their mailboxes, so you had to go in that alcove every day to look in your mailbox.

A third student reported that an Albright-trained professor would sometimes open the fall semester graduate seminar—some said this course was the center of the program—by remarking, "This seminar had its beginnings at Johns Hopkins many, many years ago." Yet another voice, more recent:

> I became fascinated with the lore of Albright and Hopkins and the program there. It didn't take long from talking to the other students and from reading done in class to get a feel for this legacy, and I felt privileged to be part of a school where there were personal relationships and intellectual ideas that united this group of scholars and that there was a heritage to it, it was moving through this century. So I was avid to hear anecdotes and when I met professors who may

11. See Philip J. King, *American Archaeology in the Mideast: A History of the American Schools of Oriental Research* (Philadelphia: American Schools of Oriental Research, 1983); Running and Freedman, *Albright.*

have known Albright, I would ask them did they ever hear Albright speak and what was it like?[12]

The second, and from a practical point of view perhaps a more important, reason for focusing on Albright is that he left very many of his own letters behind when he died. Hundreds of people wrote to Albright, too, and he saved those letters as well. This archive therefore offers an unusual opportunity to follow the negotiated pathways from Albright's private world of practice to his more public world of lectures, publications, and social/professional interactions.

Of course, the record is not complete. Often the other half of correspondence is missing, and I have been unsuccessful in locating it in other public archives. What remains also admits of alternative readings, not only because of textual ambiguities, but because of the power of perspective in shaping knowledge, as stated earlier. Yet, because of Albright's thoroughness, his papers include carbon copies of outgoing letters that often can be matched with letters received from others. It has proved possible therefore to reconstruct much of the conversation related to the incidents I describe in my essays.

My view is further limited because I pose specific questions arising out of my own philosophical orientation and social situation. I ask distinctly postmodern questions about ideology and politics, and how these dimensions of human experience provide a setting for scholarly practice in a social world of contest, inclusion, and exclusion. Moreover, for reasons already stated, I begin with the premise that neither those who appear in my narratives nor I are exempt from the ambiguities of personal choice and commitment, despite long years of training which have taught us to efface our subject positions in the language of scholarly discourse. Thus, I try to write myself into the narrative so as to make clear my belief that the creation of knowledge, then and now, has to do with contested perspectives on what the world gives us. Then and now, scholarly knowledge adds up to socially constructed facts and meaning, energized by ideological purpose and serving to support or oppose formations of social power.

12. Transcripts of interviews with graduates of Harvard University, program in Near Eastern Languages and Civilizations, conducted by Burke O. Long.

2 THE PLANTING AND REAPING OF ALBRIGHT

Shortly after her husband's death, Mrs. Emily Wright received a handwritten letter of condolence from David Noel Freedman. It was December of 1974. Freedman had recently returned home from the annual meeting of the Biblical Colloquium, a group of scholars that George Ernest Wright, the deceased, had mobilized some twenty-five years earlier and knit into an energetic presence among American biblical scholars. A younger colleague and longtime friend of Wright (they were both former students of W. F. Albright), Freedman grieved especially over Wright's absence during that fall's gathering. "Of all his numberless contributions to colleagues and students," Freedman wrote, "the creation of this learned society was one of the least known and most valuable. To me and many others, it was an ongoing seminar which provided stimulus and reward, a sense of belonging to the genuine establishment of academic excellence and intellectual adventure."[1]

In its first decade of life, 1950–59, this "learned society" was indeed a remarkable phenomenon, but not entirely for the reasons that Freedman gave. A private, by-invitation-only group, the Colloquium lived alongside the Society of Biblical Literature and Exegesis, the oldest and largest professional association of biblical scholars in America. Virtually all the Colloquium's earliest members were former students of William Foxwell Albright (increasingly, after the first decade, the circle broadened). Almost all had

1. David Noel Freedman to Emily Wright, December 21, 1974, Correspondence, David Noel Freedman (hereafter cited as CDNF; quotes by permission of David Noel Freedman).

suffered the rigors, excitement, and indignities of graduate training with a scholar of forceful personality and awesome intellectual powers.[2] Perpetuating, or even trying to re-create, some of their common experiences in the Johns Hopkins Oriental Seminary, members of the Colloquium met once a year, read research papers, and threw themselves into energetic debates. As Freedman later recalled, they submitted themselves and their researches to something like gladiatorial combat.[3] Some of their works were published in more public forums, including the then foremost American venue for technical biblical criticism, the *Journal of Biblical Literature* (Freedman was editor from 1955 to 1959) and the *Biblical Archaeologist*, a popular magazine that Wright founded in 1938 and edited for many years. As a corporate entity, the Colloquium aggressively purveyed its newly created knowledge by establishing liaisons with such commercial publishing houses as Harper's and Doubleday, advancing subsidies to authors, and by reprinting and distributing several of Albright's less technical and widely influential works.

Freedman eulogized Wright as the "Founding Father of the Biblical Colloquium" and its "catalytic agent, the galvanizing force [and] central figure and guiding genius" behind what he called a "learned society."[4] True enough, but the situation appears to me to have been more complicated. In 1980, while planning a meeting around the theme "Archaeology and the Religion of Israel" to celebrate the seminar's thirtieth anniversary, Freedman invoked Albright, not Wright, as the Colloquium's guiding spirit.[5] It was no exaggeration. While Albright only occasionally attended meetings, his work and inspiration were frequently a part of the proceedings, and some members referred to themselves as the "Albright" or "Baltimore" school.[6] In practice, membership at first was restricted to students of Albright or to those judged sympathetic to his scholarly orientation.[7]

<hr />

2. See the accounts, warmed with middle-age nostalgia, in Leona Glidden Running and David Noel Freedman, *William Foxwell Albright: A Twentieth-Century Genius* (New York: Morgan Press, 1975).

3. "G. Ernest Wright: scholar, teacher, Christian." Memorial Minute for G. Ernest Wright. *Minutes*, Biblical Colloquium, November 1974. From the files of David Noel Freedman, who for many years served as Secretary-Treasurer of the Colloquium. The official records (hereafter cited as RBC) are now with Edward Campbell, McCormick Theological Seminary, Chicago.

4. Memorial Minute.

5. Freedman to Baruch Levine, ca. January 1980; also Freedman to Yigael Yadin, January 12, 1980, CDNF.

6. George Mendenhall to William Foxwell Albright, November 6, 1952; also, Freedman to Albright, January 12, 1949. Albright Papers, American Philosophical Society, Philadelphia. Unless otherwise noted, all cited letters may be found in this archive.

7. Guests were invited to read a scholarly paper, participate in the discussions, and, if later approved without dissent, were welcomed into the Colloquium. After a few years, tensions

Fig. 1. William Foxwell Albright in his study at the Oriental Seminary, the Johns Hopkins University, ca. 1950. Courtesy of the Ferdinand Hamburger, Jr., Archives of the Johns Hopkins University.

Yet, during those early years the assembled scholars never seemed able to decide whether Albright (the "old man" as they affectionately called him)

surrounding membership, attendance, and ideological identification with Albright apparently began to create discomfort for some of the participants. Freedman suggested more openness in 1956, noting that a general delinquency in attendance may have been "induced by too heavy a concentration of Baltimore boys" (Freedman to John Bright, October 21, 1956). A dispute arose in 1960 over a scholar whose membership had been proposed, voted, then later *un*voted, and finally—this came with outside legal advice—allowed to stand. The experience led the group to codify more precisely its procedures and qualifications for membership, and at the same time to open its ranks to Catholic and Jewish scholars. By then, Albright had retired from active teaching, and the issue of a member's relationship to him or his scholarship had lost some of its urgency. (*Minutes*, Biblical Colloquium, November 26, 1961; see the report "Guiding Principles for the Selection of Members," November 25, 1961, CDNF.) The Colloquium continues to meet today, but its membership has broadened considerably and, like the field of biblical studies, members' interests have become quite diverse.

was a member or a guest.[8] He seemed to be both, and neither. A younger observer at one of the meetings Albright attended—it would have been in the mid-1960s—recalled that "as people arrived, he [Albright] was over in one area by the reception room, and they went up to him like sons returning to the patriarchal father to greet him, and he would greet each one of them. I mean it was an extraordinary scene." It was clear to this guest that the lore he had absorbed at Harvard contained an important truth: Albright had engendered in his students a "great love, and that was very much a part of who they continued to be."

It seems a love tinged with all the reverent and awe-filled complications of patriarchy. A student of Frank Cross, one of the Colloquium's first members, reported many years later that "Cross revered Albright, and he even told us that he never published anything that disagreed with Albright until after Albright died, out of respect for Albright." Another recalled that Cross frequently told his students that "Albright always said that his greatest disappointment in life was his students. My experience has been just the opposite."[9]

An artifact from the Colloquium's business of 1971 gathered many of these ambiguities into a single icon of patriarchy. Published at the top of a membership list was the name "William Foxwell Albright," splendidly set apart by asterisks from the twenty-five numbered and alphabetically ordered names that followed. Albright had been assigned no number. The progenitor ruled over the clan, or at least the Colloquium, and the text announced, to paraphrase the Bible, "These are the generations of Albright."[10]

During the first decade of its existence, the Biblical Colloquium gave social form to this culture of deference and, as will become clear, to an ideologically charged devotion to Albright with its attendant impulse to raise up grandsons of Albright. This characterization seems especially apt for Ernest Wright, whom Freedman described as "one of the great W. F. Albright's first students [who] became his most successful salesman," and who, first at McCormick Seminary, and later at Harvard Divinity School, produced "new generations of hoplites [students of Albright at Johns Hopkins] in the great army of the biblical archaeological crusade."[11] The surviving correspondence, however, suggests that Wright was not the only Colloquium

8. Mrs. Emily (G. Ernest) Wright to Burke O. Long, February 5, 1991.

9. Transcripts of interviews with graduates of the Harvard program in Near Eastern Languages and Civilizations, 1994. Hereafter cited as Interviews, NELC.

10. RBC.

11. Memorial Minute.

member who could have been so admired, if not so lavishly. Virtually all of those whom Wright had singled out for membership in the Colloquium had sent, and would continue to send, students to Albright for graduate training. Later, as the axis shifted from Baltimore and Johns Hopkins to Cambridge and Harvard, promising students would be sent to study with Wright and Cross, and from there out into their first academic posts, where some of them would, at least in part, tend the Albrightean network.

In the mid-1970s, one graduate of the Harvard program reported that scholars from the Colloquium or otherwise tied to Albright "cycled through all the time, not necessarily as guest lecturers either, just visitors on a regular basis and always to Frank Cross." Another student from the time was remembered, not only as brilliant, but as one of several who would be singled out in a "succession of fair-haired children." Besides, "he came with a pedigree, he was both a son and a grandson [of Albright]" because he had studied with one of the original members of the Colloquium.[12] There were some discussions during these years about placing new graduates strategically, so as to have the Albrightean way implanted as far afield as possible in the leading centers of biblical research.[13]

As will become clear, I view the Biblical Colloquium as a powerful social mechanism, unrivaled for its time, through which elements of a recognizable

12. Interviews, NELC.
13. In the early 1960s, Freedman and Albright observed with pleasure the concentration of scholars with Albrightean credentials at Pittsburgh Theological Seminary. Besides Freedman and James Kelso, who had worked with Albright since the 1930s, they noted James Irvine and Sidney Hills, students of Freedman and Wright, respectively, who took their Ph.D.'s with Albright; Edward Grohman, Ph.D. with Albright; and Herbert Huffmon, who had studied with Wright and Cross at McCormick Seminary, then with Albright, finally taking his Ph.D. with Mendenhall. (Albright to Freedman, September 11, 1961, Freedman to Albright, September 13, 1961.) Shortly after receiving his appointment to Harvard Divinity School in 1957, Frank Cross (according to Freedman) expressed a wish to bring Ernest Wright, and then George Mendenhall, to the faculty if the administration could be persuaded to create two positions from the impending retirement of Robert Pfeiffer. Freedman enthusiastically imagined the possibility: "That would make a tremendous team, and give real promise of carrying on the Baltimore tradition." (Freedman to Albright, March 7, 1957.) Events did not work out exactly as hoped (only Wright was invited to Harvard), but within a short time anyway the biblical side of the program in Near Eastern Languages and Civilizations was staffed with scholars who had been trained directly by Albright or, somewhat later, by Cross himself. Working against this trend, however, was the independence of the Assyriologists, such as Dietz Otto Edzard, Thorkild Jacobsen, and the linguist Thomas Lambdin who, according to some of his students, kept his distance from the Baltimore school, despite having taken his Ph.D. with Albright. A Harvard student from the 1980s reported that from lore and impressions he gained a sense that "Cross wanted Yale, he wanted one of his own in there." (Transcripts of interviews with graduates, 1994.)

Albrightean way were scatter-sown, nurtured, and harvested by these thoroughly trained and socialized offspring of Albright. In their various nuanced differences from the father, they were respectful and creative sons.

Although it met with some resistance, this closely knit group of scholars enjoyed considerable success in, as Freedman wrote, the "biblical archaeology crusade." Perhaps he spoke with tongue in cheek. Wright apparently saw these men more earnestly, as the brightest and most energetic of Albright's students at the time. They were very productive researchers, and—this was especially true of Freedman and Wright—they were quite effective at organizing publishing ventures. Moreover, as Albright had done in the earlier stages of his career, they offered a way for faith and academic criticism to flourish somewhere between anti-intellectual fundamentalism and radical intellectual skepticism. In the postwar years, this moderate-conservative theological positioning seemed especially appealing to a rising generation of biblical scholars.

The Colloquium's achievements were also due in part to the absence of similar collective entrepreneurship among scholars who differed fundamentally with Albright. Perhaps just as important, and surely not to be underestimated, was the crusading zeal of some participants, who emerge now from the faded pages of old letters like a band of missionaries, baptized in a common experience at the Johns Hopkins University and set ablaze with the rightness and righteousness of Albrightean Truth. Many years later, Ernest Wright declared himself in awe of this "mystery," that there could arise a teacher and a group of students "who have only one ideal in their minds, and that's to preserve *his* ideal; to preserve his identity, his ideas, his school."[14] Indeed, at the founding of the Biblical Colloquium, the consecrated sons and grandsons were summoned and sent forth to ensure that, as Ernest Wright put it, the future of biblical studies would belong to Albright.

Ancestors

Eight men, personally invited by Ernest Wright, constituted the first Biblical Colloquium.[15] They gathered at Western Theological Seminary, a Presbyte-

---

14. Running and Freedman, *Albright*, 316.

15. Actually the Colloquium had been *re*constituted for this occasion. In his personal notebook, G. Ernest Wright referred to it as the "second series" of meetings. Seven gatherings in the first series, with different participants, took place between November 1946 and October

rian school in Pittsburgh, on a snowy Thanksgiving weekend in 1950. David Noel Freedman hosted the meeting.

Five years earlier, Freedman had begun his studies with Albright, who seemed intrigued by this handsome and energetic "young converted Jew from Los Angeles with an Episcopal wife."[16] Albright thought Freedman would "make his mark, if nothing happens," but he was also somewhat wary of Freedman's "uncommon brilliancy," supposing that it might possibly be subjected to "erratic tendencies."[17] A few months later, his hesitancy vanished, Albright unreservedly recommended Freedman to James A. Kelso, president of Western Seminary. Trained in German-style historical criticism of the Bible, Kelso taught Old Testament for many years at the seminary, and

Fig. 2. David Noel Freedman, ca. 1950, when he began teaching at the Western Theological Seminary. Courtesy of Benedict Freedman.

1949. (Letter, Mrs. Emily [G. Ernest] Wright to Burke O. Long, February 5, 1991.) Although Wright raised money for the group and received support from McCormick Seminary (Wright to Albright, May 17, 1949), his ambition to have the earlier "theological discussion group" produce a "series of monographs and commentaries or handbooks along Biblical theology lines" never bore fruit. Wright to Albright, November 28, 1946.

16. Albright to Cullen Story, December 24, 1945.

17. Albright to James A. Kelso, October 3, 1946.

now was within sight of retirement. He had met Albright some twenty-five years earlier in Jerusalem, when Albright directed the American School of Oriental Research and Kelso served as its annual lecturer.

Telling his Jerusalem colleague that Freedman had been "developing most remarkably," and that his "brilliance is solid and his devotion [to his work] is intensifying," Albright suggested that Freedman would be a nearly ideal choice for the seminary faculty.[18] Some months later, Freedman recalled, Kelso traveled to Johns Hopkins where he and Albright jointly interviewed this young and "nearly ideal choice." Within the year, carrying accolades of promise with his fresh Ph.D., Freedman joined the faculty in Pittsburgh. Right away he began to forge a strategic link between this new school and the one he had left in Baltimore.

Long before Freedman arrived, however, Albright had established other ties to Pittsburgh. Across the Allegheny River, and just a few neighborhoods away, was Pittsburgh-Xenia Theological Seminary, a Presbyterian school created in 1930 when the evangelical Xenia Theological Seminary of St. Louis merged with the Theological Seminary of the United Presbyterian Church in Pittsburgh.[19] At that time James L. Kelso (not the Kelso who headed Western Seminary), a graduate of Xenia-St. Louis and member of its faculty since 1923, moved to Pittsburgh and began to teach Old Testament to ministers-in-training at the new school. Kelso had studied with Melvin Grove Kyle, who, as president of the St. Louis–based Xenia in the 1920s, had befriended the young Albright, promoted his career, and greatly aided the archaeological work of the American School in Jerusalem. As assistant field director of the Kyle/Albright excavations at Tell Beit Mirsim in British Mandate Palestine, Kelso first met Albright.

In those early days, President Kyle played a key role in Albright's initial successes as director of the Jerusalem school. Despite great differences in age and academic training, about which Albright was cautious and diplomatic, they admired each other, and each seemed to benefit from the other's position and particular talents.[20] Albright offered Kyle the prestige of ar-chaeological excavations, and Kyle offered Albright financial backing and a forum in the evangelical Christian community.

---

18. Albright to James A. Kelso, March 9, 1947.

19. J. and S. Ohles, *Private Colleges and Universities II* (Westport, Conn.: Greenwood, 1982), 982–83; James A. Walther, ed., *Ever a Frontier: The Bicentennial History of Pittsburgh Theological Seminary* (Grand Rapids: Eerdmans, 1994), 117–58.

20. See Albright, "In Memoriam: Melvin Grove Kyle," *Bulletin of the American Schools of Oriental Research* 51 (September 1933): 5–7 (hereafter cited as *BASOR*). Also, Albright to father, May 15, 1921.

Fig. 3.   The staff at Tell Beit Mirsim excavation, ca. 1932. Front row (left to right): James L. Kelso, Albright, Melvin Grove Kyle, and Nelson Glueck. Second row (fourth from the left), John Bright. Courtesy of Leona Running.

During a three-week term in 1921 as guest lecturer at the Jerusalem school, Kyle recognized Albright's academic promise. He also admired the young scholar's evangelical Christian convictions and inclination to accept the Bible as historically trustworthy. Kyle found an ally in Albright's guarded willingness—Albright was much more reserved than Kyle in this respect— to proffer archaeological findings in support of the Bible. Kyle edited *Bibliotheca Sacra*, a journal of decidedly evangelical conviction, and used its pages tirelessly to promote Albright and biblical archaeology in the service of Christian apologetics.[21] He raised money for Albright's exploration of

21. See, for example, Kyle's early article, "The Recent Testimony of Archaeology to the Scriptures" *Bibliotheca Sacra* 67 (1910): 373–90 (hereafter cited as *BS*). In 1925 Kyle and his editors instituted a "Quarterly Review of the Archaeological World," in which the latest findings were blended with religious belief, burnished with science and romanticism, and published as confirmation of the biblical version of ancient history. Kyle, given to exaggeration, pressed Albright's words far beyond what Albright himself would have wished, or would have stated so unabashedly. Of Albright's report about excavations at Tel El Ful (see *BASOR* 7 [1922]: 7–8),

the Dead Sea Valley, and publicized the results of this and subsequent excavations, many of which were joint ventures of the American School and Xenia Theological Seminary. All these expeditions were supported, as Albright later wrote, largely with money earned by Kyle's "indefatigable writing and lecturing."[22] It was likely Kyle who introduced Albright to the Fleming H. Revell Company, a prominent publishing house for evangelical Christian readers. Earlier, this company had issued Kyle's account of the Xenia-ASOR explorations of Sodom and Gomorrah,[23] and it later published Albright's first book on the Bible and archaeology, which drew upon the Kyle/Albright excavations at Tell Beit Mirsim.[24] Kyle lavishly praised this book and its author on the pages of *Bibliotheca Sacra*.[25]

After Kyle's death, his student James L. Kelso, a Presbyterian minister and Kyle/Albright protégé, kept the evangelical spirit of Kyle's seminary flowing

---

Kyle wrote: "It does not give us much information; it simply parallels the Biblical account of Gibea of Saul. But the exact confirmation of that story, as set forth by Dr. Albright, is but another illustration of the trustworthiness of ancient documents, of which he is a strenuous advocate." (*BS* 82 [1925]: 11–12.) Of their work together, Kyle wrote to Albright, "Our expedition [in search of biblical Zoar] has made a great stir, only second to Tut Ankh Amen, though far behind that yet. But Dr. Montgomery gave a notice to the Associated Press and it went like wild fire. Not only as news but also in the editorial column. I hope we may find enough to warrant all that has been said." (Kyle to Albright, November 29, 1923.) See also *BS* 84 (1927): 6–8. In 1929 Kyle excitedly played to an ardent public, declaring that "Archaeological copy is avidly sought by the daily press as well as the great popular journals. Despite the blatant outcry of unbelief against the Bible, the great populace of the Christian world desires to know *that the Bible is true* and so welcomes everything that tends to corroborate it." (*BS* 86 [1929]: 8; italics in original.) See also *BS* 88 (1931): 15. Albright's more moderate assurances to evangelical readers may be seen in an early article, "Archaeological Discovery in the Holy Land," *BS* 79 (1922): 401–17.

22. W. F. Albright, "In Memoriam: Melvin Grove Kyle," *BASOR* 51 (September 1933): 6. For examples of Kyle's reporting, see, for the "cities of the plain," *BS* 81 (1924): 276–79; on Tell Beit Mirsim, see vols. 83 (1926), 378–402; 85 (1928), 381–408; 89 (1932), 393–419. Each issue of *BS* carried a regular feature, "Archaeological Reviews," through which Kyle popularized the latest discoveries, often with an application to questions of dogmatic truth or defenses against "modernist" thinking about the Bible.

23. *Explorations at Sodom: The Story of Sodom in the Light of Modern Research* (New York: Fleming H. Revell Co., 1928).

24. *The Archaeology of Palestine and the Bible* (New York: Fleming H. Revell Co., 1932). In 1927, Kyle told Albright that Revell had requested a book on "Kirjath Sepher" (Tell Beit Mirsim), and that despite reservations (at the time they had much more excavating to do), he proposed that they quickly produce something like "A Book from Book-Town," a title that played on the translation of *Kiryath Seper*. "I fear there would not be much money in it, but it would make our work known—and—help get the money [for the continuing excavations]." Albright recorded his response on the top of the page: "answered 4/28 hastily in appreciation." Kyle to Albright, April 13, 1927. I have been unable to trace the incident further, but since the Revell Company published nothing on Tell Beit Mirsim under Kyle's name, it is reasonable to assume that Albright's first book was the outcome of this early conversation.

25. *BS* 89 (1932): 246–47.

through Pittsburgh to Baltimore and Albright. Although he never took formal instruction from Albright, Kelso was clearly an admiring disciple. From letters written during the 1930s and 1940s, Kelso seems a diffident, nearly awestruck friend and colleague of Albright (they were less than a year apart in age but Kelso often concluded his letters with "your friend and pupil," or the like[26]). And like a missionary brandishing success, Kelso enthusiastically wrote that his Pittsburgh-Xenia students were "all converts to arch. & it's [*sic*] ideals of Bible study."[27] Kelso dreamed of writing a series of books on the Old Testament, "provided I can get them past you as a board of censorship,"[28] and he once asked Albright to nominate him for membership in the Society of Biblical Literature.[29] Just five months shy of his fifty-first birthday, and apparently at the urging of Pittsburgh-Xenia's new president, also an admirer of Albright, Kelso sought advice on taking a Ph.D. at Johns Hopkins.[30]

Albright encouraged Kelso in all these aspirations, and in effect culti-vated a strong, sympathetic Albrightean presence among the evangelical Presbyterians in Pittsburgh. Telling Kelso that "we need more conservatives to offset a strong liberal slant in the Society,"[31] Albright supported his membership in the Society of Biblical Literature. He was also pleased with Kelso's developing, self-taught expertise in metallurgy, and he especially encouraged the use of such a "hard" science to explain obscurities in the biblical text.[32]

Albright was so impressed by Kelso's scientific work—it was a harbinger of techniques that would become prevalent among archaeologists later in the twentieth century—that he encouraged him to take a Ph.D. at Johns Hopkins. On the strength of his "remarkable research in ceramics and other technical branches [of archaeology]," Kelso's status had been completely altered, Albright wrote in 1943. Allowing appropriate credit for previous accomplishments, and envisioning only a technical dissertation (Kelso lacked

26. Kelso to Albright, March 14, 1941; January 8, 1943.

27. Kelso to Albright, February 19, 1943.

28. Kelso to Albright, November 11, 1941.

29. Kelso to Albright, October 6, 1941.

30. Kelso to Albright, May 16, 1943. See also George Long, president of Pittsburgh-Xenia, to Albright, September 17, 1943. The year before taking up his post, Long probably encountered Albright when studying with John Bright at Union Theological Seminary in Richmond, Virginia. See Kelso to Albright, December 29, 1942.

31. Albright to Kelso, October 8, 1941. See also Albright to Kelso, November 30, 1941.

32. Albright to Kelso, January 22, 1943; Kelso to Albright, May 25 and June 14, 1943. Albright told Ernest Wright that Kelso "will soon become our foremost authority on the natural scientific aspects of archaeology" (Albright to Wright, February 3, 1944).

the linguistic training that Albright normally insisted on for his students), Albright added, "I can promise you a Ph.D., I think, in one year."[33]

Although nothing came of these hopes, Albright and Kelso continued regular consultations and collaborated on research papers, including the official reports on Albright's excavations at Tell Beit Mirsim.[34] As late as 1955, they were still working closely with one another as Kelso prepared his own technical reports on the excavations at Bethel.[35]

When David Noel Freedman joined the faculty at Western Seminary in 1948, it is easy to imagine the spirits of Kyle-Kelso-Albright, the forefathers in a sense, wandering and mingling through this evangelical Presbyterian space in Pittsburgh.[36] Two years later, on that snowy Thanksgiving weekend, a generation of much more recent descent from Albright constituted themselves as the Biblical Colloquium.

Sons and Grandsons

Six of the men, all teachers of the Old Testament in Protestant theological schools, had written their doctoral dissertations under Albright. George Ernest Wright, the convener, received his Ph.D. in 1937 and now taught at McCormick Seminary in Chicago. John Bright, of Union Theological Seminary in Richmond, graduated in 1940. George Mendenhall, Ph.D. 1947, taught at Hamma Divinity School, Wittenberg College. David Noel Freedman, host of the meeting, collected his degree in 1948. Frank Moore Cross,

---

33. Albright to Kelso, May 20, 1943.

34. Perhaps more than any other, this expedition established Albright as the foremost authority in archaeological matters, for in this work, he set the typology—classification of artifacts by style and historical period—by which everyone for a long time would date layers of human occupation at ancient city sites. Kelso co-authored a chapter in *The Excavation of Tell Beit Mirsim, III: The Iron Age* (ASOR vols. 21–23; New Haven: American Oriental Society, 1943).

35. Kelso to Albright, August 9, 1955. For further information on Kyle-Kelso-Albright associations and biblical archaeology, all nourished by faculty and students in Pittsburgh, see Nancy Lapp, "Archaeology and the James L. Kelso Bible Lands Museum," in Walther, ed., *Ever a Frontier*, 237–62.

36. In 1959, when Pittsburgh-Xenia merged with Western Seminary, James L. Kelso became a faculty colleague of Freedman at the newly constituted Pittsburgh Theological Seminary. A short while later, Albright observed with satisfaction that with six of his former students at this seminary, the "Baltimore school" was better represented in Pittsburgh than anywhere else. (Albright to Freedman, September 11, 1961; Freedman to Albright, September 13, 1961. See note 13 above.) Soon after 1961, Grohman, Huffmon, and Irvine left Pittsburgh for positions elsewhere.

Jr., and Carl Howie had received their doctorates just a few months before the meeting. The youngest of the clan was Sidney O. Hills, who was at the time studying for his research degree with Albright. An eighth participant, Carl Umhau Wolf, of the Chicago Lutheran Seminary, took courses with Albright as a postdoctoral student in 1944, was a friend of Wright, and had participated with Wright in wartime theological discussion groups in the Chicago area.

The network of generations was actually tighter than it seems at first glance. Ernest Wright had taught Cross, then Hills, at McCormick Seminary, and sent them on to Albright; Carl Howie had been a student of John Bright at Union Theological Seminary before traveling up to Baltimore; George Mendenhall had been led to Albright by Jacob Myers, his teacher at the Gettysburg Lutheran Theological Seminary. Both of them took courses with Albright in the early postwar years, and Myers received his doctorate only a year before Mendenhall.

In 1950, most of these men were following, or about to adopt, a pattern evident in the relations established early on between Albright and Wright. They shared academic training in a university that embodied a positive valuation of science. They studied with a man who thought of himself as scientist and Christian theist, and who was convinced that science could lift human beings from their subjective darkness and set them on a meliorative course toward liberation of mind and spirit.[37] They learned from Albright how to join such ideologies of science to religious faith and how to construct a linguistic and historical setting for the Bible with, as Freedman later wrote, a "strong Christian bias, and an essentially apologetic approach to the subject of religion, especially biblical religion in (or against) its environment."[38] Albright gave his students a way to break the chains of "arid Protestant scholasticism," as John Bright later put it, and to embrace a Bible whose religious and historical claims could be accepted with rational integrity.[39]

37. Burke O. Long, "Mythic Trope in the Autobiography of Albright," *Biblical Archaeologist* 56:1 (1993): 36–45. See also Chapter 4 below.

38. David Noel Freedman, "W. F. Albright as Historian," in Gus van Beek, ed., *The Scholarship of William Foxwell Albright: An Appraisal* (Harvard Semitic Studies 33; Atlanta: Scholars Press, 1989), 35.

39. Author's interview with John Bright, June 12, 1990. In a letter to Albright, Sidney Hills wrote of his anguished encounter with modernism, loss of Christian faith, and reversion to fundamentalist denunciation of everything modern. When he at last discovered Albright's books and lectures, and particularly the way Albright built confidence in the Bible's trustworthiness, Hills wrote, he finally was able to exorcise the demons that had tormented him. (Sidney O. Hills to Albright, March 28, 1953.) Hills graduated from Johns Hopkins in 1954, and served on the

Ernest Wright particularly sought to build a new biblical theology on the basis of archaeological and historical research.[40] This bundle of attitude and purpose went hand in hand with creating an Albrightean landscape in America. "My great aim in life," Wright confided in 1949, "is to find more men like Cross, Freedman, and Hills; get them trained under you, and then into more OT positions in this country—this because that is the only way we're going to [get] OT studies back on some decent level!"[41]

Like Wright, all the first members of the Colloquium would develop their postgraduate careers under the continuing tutelage of Albright. Acting as referee, confidant, and scholarly resource, he frequently would encourage their work, particularly insofar as it reinforced and extended some of Albright's most cherished historical and theological convictions. For their part, the students seemed most content to offer themselves and their researches for Albright's approval.[42] Most of them accepted the paradigm of father begetting sons, who then begot more sons, in an affectionate bond of intellectual and generational solidarity. For his part, Albright identified closely with those of his students who carried on in his tradition, for which, according to John Bright, he invented the term "Baltimore school."[43]

As will become clear, these sons and grandsons of Albright (there would be no "daughters" in the family for many years) constituted a political force within the small world of biblical scholars. They probably also exercised considerable influence on those members of Christian churches who eagerly sought the theological and faith-building results of Albrightean-style researches.

Wright had first encountered Albright some fifteen years earlier, in 1934, when in thrall of his "tremendous, simply fascinating lectures" at the American School in Jerusalem. Wright showed promise as an innovative archaeologist and then, as he later recalled, "I had it made with Albright."[44] He had learned of Albright even before this, however, having taken a theological

faculty of Western Theological Seminary until 1959. After Western's merger with Pittsburgh-Xenia, he stayed on at the school, newly named Pittsburgh Theological Seminary, until 1975. Hills participated in the Biblical Colloquium, however, for only a few years.

40. See, above all, *The Book of the Acts of God* (Garden City, N.Y.: 1957), which Wright co-authored with Reginald H. Fuller.

41. Wright to Albright, January 24, 1949.

42. Albright's voluminous correspondence with former students amply documents this extended association, as do the testimonies of the participants. See Running and Freedman, *Albright*, 194–220.

43. See Running and Freedman, *Albright*, 198.

44. Running and Freedman, *Albright*, 202.

degree at the Presbyterian Theological Seminary (later McCormick), and had been sent on to Hopkins by Ovid Sellers, one of Albright's admiring friends and former students from Jerusalem of the late 1920s. After receiving his Ph.D. at Johns Hopkins in 1937, Wright set out on an energetic and creative path of archaeological research, but always within the orbit of Albright's mentoring presence. Albright remained for him a revered teacher and colleague. According to Yigael Yadin, Ernest Wright was Albright's "most beloved pupil."[45] He was to become the most accomplished biblical archaeologist whom Albright trained at Johns Hopkins.

Wright was also an avid evangelist for the Albrightean approach to Bible and archaeology, and for the theological offspring of this union.[46] Throughout his career, but especially in its first two decades, Wright discussed with his former teacher all manner of technical archaeological research, frequently solicited advice and correction on pending publications, took up suggestions from Albright as to topics for scholarly investigation, and reported academic gossip, notably as it was relevant to the spread of Albright's historical and theological convictions.[47] He also relied extensively on Albright's support, even contributory labors, when establishing the popularizing journal *Biblical Archaeologist*. Wright edited this publication for many years from its founding in 1938, when he wrote that it "would fill a great hole, and if properly put up, be a great success, as well as 'stealing all the thunder' in the American Archaeological world, especially in this day of picture magazines."[48] The journal presented the latest news of archaeological exploration with academic responsibility. It also became a powerful voice for Albright's view of these matters, or rather for Wright's popularizing what Freedman much later called the "biblical-archaeological crusade."[49] As late as 1960, Wright

45. ASOR *Newsletter* 3 (September 1974): 4.

46. In a 1951 assessment of Old Testament studies, Wright emphasized a return to theological questions and showed an appreciation for literary investigations of oral tradition far beyond what Albright could muster. Nevertheless, constructing (Albright's) narrative of two eras—"before archaeology" and "after archaeology"—with Albright at the turning point, Wright passed on and defended many of his teacher's most cherished theological and historical convictions. Toward the end of the article, he gazed at the future of biblical studies from the heights of the Baltimore school and saw a revitalized Old Testament study that took full account of theology and the "archaeological revolution." G. Ernest Wright, "The Study of the Old Testament," in Arnold Nash, ed., *Protestant Thought in the Twentieth Century: Whence and Whither?* (New York: Macmillan, 1951), 17–44, esp. 30–34.

47. See the numerous letters from Wright to Albright, spanning the years 1937–58.

48. Wright to Albright, November 15, 1937.

49. Millar Burrows, who along with Albright and Ephraim Speiser served on the first editorial board of *Biblical Archaeologist*, conveyed something of the general orientation and

actively sought to assure, even as changes brought by Albright's advancing age seemed inevitable, that the American Schools, and especially its *Bulletin*, would continue to reflect Albright's "line," since others "not precisely down our alley" were then occupying responsible positions in the parent organization.[50]

Convening the Biblical Colloquium in 1950, then, was one of many entrepreneurial ventures set in motion by Ernest Wright. In the urgency of strategic vision, however, he may have taken the cue from Albright himself. Often dismissing scholars for resisting the new orientation, or rather implications, he believed archaeology to have brought to biblical studies, Albright looked to his own students, especially as their numbers swelled in postwar years, to ride a surging tide of victory far up onto the shore. As World War II was drawing to a close, he had already envisioned a future for Albrightean biblical studies with at least some of the same people that Wright had in mind. "I now have a number of brilliant students," he wrote to his parents, "some of whom are carrying on better than I had hoped—so well in fact that I am no longer at all worried about seeing my views about the Bible win out."[51]

It is not surprising, then, that by late summer of 1950 Wright voiced his impatience with the discussion groups he had organized in the 1940s (the Biblical Colloquium "first series"). Telling Albright that since "the future belongs to your school of thought," Wright wrote that he planned to gather "a group of your students plus two or three others (probably Gentiles)

---

spirit of Wright's (and the American School's) founding vision: "By providing evidence for the establishment of the text and materials for the fuller understanding of the language, by lighting up the whole background so that figures of biblical history no longer move in solitude across a dark stage, by explaining many details and illustrating others, and by confirming the essential authenticity of the record, though at the same time raising new problems and correcting a detail here and there, archaeology leads the student of the Bible into an incomparably fuller understanding and deeper appreciation than was ever before possible." ("How Archaeology Helps the Student of the Bible," *Biblical Archaeologist* 3/2 [May 1940], 17.)

50. Wright to Albright, May 21, 1960. The concern was focused on the question of a successor to Albright, who had edited *BASOR* for some 30 years (he would serve for 8 more years), and had over that long time period made the journal very much a reflection of his own interests, scholarly values, and philosophical commitments, while believing, as he wrote to Herbert May, that "BASOR is strictly neutral ground" with regard to biblical theological issues. (Albright to Herbert G. May, August 12, 1942.) See Delbert Hillers, "Fifty Years of the Bulletin of the American Schools of Oriental Research," *BASOR* 200 (December 1970): 5.

51. Albright to parents, December 22, 1946. He probably had in mind at least Mendenhall, Cross, and Freedman. Mendenhall had resumed his studies at the Oriental Seminary of Johns Hopkins University following his war service with the U.S. Navy; Freedman began in 1945; Cross came to Hopkins the following year.

for at least a yearly meeting."[52] He wanted to keep together "the most promising" of Albright's students ("your group," he called them) and harness their energies for a series of joint projects.[53] As John Bright much later recalled, "Ernest Wright decided on a lot of things that were needed at the time . . . and he farmed some of them out. That's the way I got started on my *History*."[54]

It seemed that some of Wright's frustrated hopes for the "first series" of Colloquium meetings might at last be realized. Moreover, a now defunct theological dictionary of the Bible which he and Albright had planned with Westminster Press in 1944–45 might be revived.[55] Besides the lexicon and a history of ancient Israel, Wright had in mind at least two other tasks for the group: a Wright-Cross introduction to the Bible,[56] and a series of Old Testament commentaries.

In retrospect, it is clear that such ambitions, if realized, would have created distinctively American alternatives in a field dominated by European and English classics belonging to an earlier generation. None of the great compendiums of biblical knowledge in 1950 took full advantage of the Christian theological possibilities of Albright's emphasis on archaeology and comparative philology; and none save Albright, among those who approached the Bible historically and critically, so tirelessly defended the Bible's historical trustworthiness.

Frank Cross, Wright's student at McCormick Seminary, shared this boldly reformist vision, which apparently derived from Albright. Reporting his first impressions of Wellesley College—it was his first full-time teaching appointment—Cross wrote to Albright that he planned to "corrupt" the students with some "facts and disgracefully Albrightean ideas." He had

52. Albright often pointed with pride to a mix of Jewish and Christian students at the Oriental Seminary at Hopkins, and Wright himself was a part of that cooperative atmosphere in the late 1930s despite strident anti-Semitic voices in America at the time. I would guess that his exclusionary qualifier, "probably Gentiles," stemmed from his keen interest in Christian theology, and his hope that this "Albright group" would publish studies of the Bible that had strong relevance to Christian theology and church practice.

53. Wright to Albright, August 2, 1950.

54. Transcript of interview, Burke O. Long with John Bright, 1991. The standard work of biblical history in English was already nearly twenty years old: W. O. E. Oesterley and T. H. Robinson, *A History of Israel*, 2 vols. (Oxford: Clarendon Press, 1932).

55. The idea was similar in concept to Gerhard Kittel and G. Friedrich, eds., *Theologisches Wörterbuch zum Neuen Testament* (Stuttgart: Kohlhammer, from 1933).

56. Major works then available included Robert Pfeiffer, *Introduction to the Old Testament*, 2d ed. (Cambridge: Harvard University Press, 1948) and Otto Eissfeldt, *Einleitung in das Alte Testament* (Tübingen: J. C. B. Mohr, 1934).

Fig. 4.   G. Ernest Wright, 1958. Courtesy of the Harvard University Archives.

found only one supportive colleague at Wellesley in "our battle against the pie-eyed Pfeiffer of Harvard and local followers." But—it seems now as though he were opening a campaign to win the students' minds—he reported that he had made multiple copies of Albright's works available for student assignments. "You have occasionally let remarks drop about the sad state of Biblical studies in America," Cross wrote. "Anything you may have said (or even thought) was overly mild."[57]

Cross was excited about plans for the Colloquium's first meeting, then just two months away. Delighted that he and others were "getting down to concerted action," he speculated about the coming new order. "With the pioneer work and syntheses performed by you," he wrote, "even those of us who are limited should be able to produce solid work and fill the vacuum which now exists in almost every category of handbook." He, like Wright, looked for revolution, and with just a hint of apocalyptic fervor looked for

57. Cross to Albright, September 27, 1950; see also Cross to Albright, August 19, 1950.

Fig. 5. Frank Moore Cross, Jr., 1957. Courtesy of the Harvard University Archives.

it to build a new order on the ruins of decadence. "Perhaps," he continued, "the revolution in OT thought and theology will be sooner than some of these particularly depressing experiences [at Wellesley] lead one to think."

When Albright was told of Wright's plans, he was pleased, but refused an invitation to participate in the Colloquium's first meeting.[58] He asserted that the new enterprise should preserve its "priceless possession" of independence. Yet Wright had asked for advice on membership, since he could not include all of Albright's recent students among the "most promising"; and there was at least the possibility of inviting a few scholars who had no direct ties to Albright, he thought.

Herbert May of the graduate school of theology at Oberlin College should not be considered, Albright responded in the same letter, having just championed the Colloquium's independence. He was "too much tarred with a kind of Chicago proto-philosophy . . . to understand and sympathize

58. Wright to Albright, August 2, 1950.

fully with us." Another scholar, J. Philip Hyatt of Vanderbilt Divinity School, could not "see the point of our theological approach" and, besides, his "Yale training prevents him from utilizing the archaeological data adequately." Even though they perhaps were sympathetic to Albright's orientation, May and Hyatt had not been trained sufficiently in his methods and his convictions about the power of conclusions to be drawn from archaeological excavations. Herbert May perhaps was especially problematic for Albright. He had studied with John M. P. Smith of the University of Chicago and was still associated fairly closely with that university. As will be seen, these ties located May on the margins of Albright's notion of scientific progress. Besides, to Albright both men waved the flags of liberal Protestantism and pursued mostly literary, rather than archaeological, study of the Bible.

Some concern had even been raised about the suitability of Carl Howie for the group.[59] In response, Albright admitted to Howie's philological carelessness, but defended him as ammunition in a war.

> In collaboration with John Bright I think he [Howie] will produce some good work, since Bright is as meticulous as Howie is careless in detail. . . . The followers of Torrey, Irwin, etc., will have a very hard time answering Howie [on his analysis of the Book of Ezekiel], and will take it out on snide criticisms of irrelevant matters. I am very happy to have this addition to our arsenal.[60]

59. Freedman and Cross at the time were discussing several projects that Albright was planning, which, according to Albright's usual practice, would involve assistance of various kinds from current and former students. "The whole business will require a good deal of thought and some serious discussion," Freedman wrote, a little conspiratorially. "I am a little worried about Howie's crawling into the inner circle, and we may have to take drastic steps." (Freedman to Frank Moore Cross, Jr., July 12, 1950, CDNF.) After the second meeting of the Colloquium, Howie's suitability was still being discussed following what Wright described as a "terrible" presentation by the "weakest link" in the Albrightean group. Although he had earlier acquiesced to Albright's urging that Howie become a member, Wright now felt that "the sincerity and depth of Howie's scholarly interest" were so suspect as to pose a distinct problem. "We cannot have that sort of stuff in our group," he wrote, "if it is to keep going and excited about what it is doing." Howie was better suited to the ministry or college teaching, Wright thought. (Wright to John Bright, November 20, 1951. Courtesy of Charles Bright.) A little later, Howie took up a pastorate and permanently left academic life.

60. Albright to George Ernest Wright, August 8, 1950. Albright's caricature of the (his) opponents to Howie's dissertation apparently found its way into Wright's Albright-centered assessment of the "whence and whither" of biblical studies. On studies of Ezekiel, he dismissed what Albright dismissed, and approved of Howie's work as a "scholarly defense of the older conservative view [of literary composition] from the Albright school, and one that will be difficult to answer except by the critique of marginal matters." See Wright, "The Study of the Old Testament," 28–29, n. 5. (See note 46 above.)

An Ideological Map

Weaponry in a struggle to hasten the triumph of Albright's way—the metaphor was a favorite with Albright and his students during these years. It had its setting in a narrative that may be pieced together from repeated themes and motifs, fragments of assessment, and miscellaneous remarks about scholars and the fields in which Albright worked. In their cumulative iteration, these comments suggest a rather encompassing viewpoint that Albright frequently invoked in simplified form to ground himself and his values in the authorizing paradigms of science.

An older world of biblical criticism is passing away, Albright often stated. It is a world populated by workers so caught up in arid debates about literary forms, textual history, and authors of biblical documents that they are unable to use effectively those artifactual and inscriptional data which now permit fresh understandings of the Bible. A new era approaches, indeed has already dawned, and in these latter days Albright and his students hasten the victory of a new vision of biblical studies. They will reclaim the Bible from religious skeptics and myopic literary theorists; they will present a Bible that is finally explained in its ancient context, and yet a Bible that is historically reliable and theologically relevant to a modern world; they will grasp and master a Bible scientifically with the aid of philology and archaeological discoveries.

To the waning age belong paradigmatic characters against which Albright repeatedly rang the changes of the times: the nineteenth-century scholar Julius Wellhausen, and his twentieth-century American heirs, Robert Pfeiffer of Harvard (the "pie-eyed Pfeiffer" according to the young Cross), William Irwin of the University of Chicago (whom Albright would privately dismiss as "no scholar at all"),[61] and C. C. Torrey (whose dissembling followers, Albright said, would oppose Howie's studies of Ezekiel). All these characters, like Albright and his students, submitted to the Enlightenment-inspired myths of scientific modernity—I mean, for example, the supremacy of a master knower, a self-conscious self using reason to reach truth; the conviction that human language, if stripped of its subjective confusions, can describe the objective world-out-there. Yet these workers of the waning age are no longer modern, or scientific, enough for Albright. They are inadequately trained in the study of comparative Semitic languages, and unenlightened by the new archaeology. These interpreters of the Bible, so the narrative goes, pursue arid methods of documentary study of the Bible.

---

61. Albright to Erwin R. Goodenough, July 3, 1939.

They spin elaborate variations on Julius Wellhausen's theories about how original documents were combined over time by ancient authors and editors to make up a composite biblical text. Moreover, they devalue the grandeur of ancient Hebraic religion. These workers toil in subjective isolation; they are blind to innovative progress that is purchased by more scientifically gathered information increasingly available from the artifacts of field archaeology. Biblical criticism is in need of a prophetlike reformation, and, enmeshed with it, Christianity is in need of defense and renewal.

Indeed, when he began his graduate training Albright described himself as ready to take up a "crusade," to employ the tools of scientific philology and archaeological investigation to reclaim biblical truth that had been lost, denied, or obscured by a verdant growth of misguided researches.[62] At midcareer, he saw himself more in terms of a Protestant Reformer, one who was leading a renaissance of modern times. Skeletal notes from lectures delivered at Gettysburg Seminary in May 1944—the words were penciled on the back side of an elegantly printed invitation to the event—suggest something of the sweeping narrative in which Albright located himself on a map of modern study of the Bible.[63]

The first lecture was entitled, "The O.T. [Old Testament] After a Century of Progress." Implying a familiar plot of scientific advances, Albright spoke of an "established order" constantly having to adjust under the impact of new information. Knowledge about the Bible had passed through a "philological phase"—study of the biblical text in the shadow of the European enlightenment, but framed in the nineteenth and twentieth centuries first by Hegelian dialectics, then by comparative science of religions, then by theories of written sources. These perspectives had now been rendered obsolete by a new order, the "archaeological phase" of biblical research. Those scholars who represented the before-archaeological achievements on this timeline of philological advancement—the lecture notes mention Julius Wellhausen and Hermann Gunkel—belong to a bygone era. Wellhausen's heirs, Robert Pfeiffer and William Irwin, even though still working at leading research institutions in what Albright called the "current situation," are relegated to obsolescence at the margins of progress. The "archaeological phase" is taking hold and is creating a new "synthesis to our day."

Of course, the primary voice was Albright's. He constructed the narrative and provided the triumphal interpretation of its central character, the Bible

62. For a fuller description of Albright as religious apologist, see Chapter 4, below.
63. Original in Albright Papers.

as scientific object. And he apparently concluded, as so many of his publications did, by locating himself at the cusp of that wave of progress: "As I view the O.T."

The second lecture, entitled "What Does the O.T. Mean for Us Today?" apparently construed archaeology and comparative Semitic philology as decisive influences in the history of Christian appropriation of the Bible. An overgrowth of ecclesiastical tradition early on "eclipsed" the original scriptures of the Church with "outgrown tradition." However, the Protestant Reformation cut away such tradition by appealing directly to unencumbered Scripture—the lecture notes mention "the reformation and the Bible"—and thus prepared the way for modern historical and literary studies of the Bible. This "higher criticism" of both the Old and New Testaments presumably transmuted the reformation desire for paradigmatic beginnings into a scientific quest for original text and first meanings. However, both Testaments were eclipsed, "overgrown by tradition," until archaeology and philology arose. Yet another reforming impulse has thus shaped a "renaissance of our day," in which one can gain encumbered access to the original biblical text. Without such a modern reformation, or prophetic recovery, Albright seemed to imply, the question, "What does the O.T. mean for us today?" could hardly be answered, at least not correctly.

Considering his prominence among biblical archaeologists at the time, Albright's implication would have been clear to his audience: Albright the archaeologist, Albright the unrivaled master of comparative philology, Albright the reformer, not only told the tale, but made the tale possible. He recovered truth that, recalling the phrase he used as a young man, had been "muffled and smoked by accumulated misunderstandings."[64]

Embedded in this reformist narrative was a map of scholarly territory in which flesh-and-blood Old Testament scholars seemed to represent ideological struggles. Despite Albright's unquestioning acceptance of the main lines of Julius Wellhausen's "higher criticism," such as the theory of multiple authorship and complex editorial history of the Pentateuch,[65] Wellhausen took form in Albright's mythic narrative as archantagonist. Failing to take

64. Albright to his mother, Zephine Viola Foxwell Albright, December 26, 1913.
65. This dependence is very clear in *From the Stone Age to Christianity: Monotheism and the Historical Process* (Baltimore: Johns Hopkins University Press, 1940), even to accepting Wellhausen's scheme of relative dating for the posited documents J, E, D, and P. Having suggested his basic agreement for many years, Albright explicitly confirmed it in "The Ancient Near East and the Religion of Israel," *Journal of Biblical Literature* 59 (1940): 95, n. 13. See also "A Revision of Early Hebrew Chronology," *Journal of the Palestine Oriental Society* 1 (1921): 50.

very much account of the late nineteenth-century stirrings of nascent archaeology, Wellhausen symbolized a tradition of literary and philological
scholarship which Albright characterized as inward-looking, self-referential,
and finally unscientific, because it did not look to the results of archaeology
for solutions to literary problems. Wellhausen employed an evolutionary
view of historical development; Albright, while adopting his own form of
evolutionism, labeled Wellhausen a "Hegelian" and thought he had imposed
a rigid dialectical scheme on cultural history.

On the basis of literary-historical analysis, Wellhausen drew some conclusions that, when Albright reduced them to a few theologicohistorical
issues, left him viscerally disturbed. For example, traditions about the earliest Hebrew ancestors, according to Wellhausen, were for the most part
creations of a much later age and thus were historically unreliable. As seen
above, Albright presumed, and often asserted confirmation of a historically
trustworthy Bible. Moreover, because these ancestral traditions were written
so late, claimed Wellhausen, they obscured the primitivity of religious and
intellectual development that characterized the ancestral Hebrew people.
Thus, credit for achieving the high ethical monotheism to which Christianity
was heir belonged not to Abraham or Moses, but to their later descendants,
the great Old Testament prophets. From an early age, Albright believed that
authentic monotheism had begun with Moses, and that the biblical prophets
were rather less innovators than reformers who called for restoration of the
pure Mosaic ideals in an age that threatened their dissolution.[66]

Robert Pfeiffer of Harvard held a place in Albright's implied narrative because he represented the mid-twentieth-century legacy of a before-
archaeology Wellhausen. Despite their very similar educations—Pfeiffer

66. See Julius Wellhausen, *Prolegomena to the History of Ancient Israel* (Edinburgh: A & C
Black, 1885; trans. from the 1878 ed.). Albright set forth his opposition to Wellhausen's constructions of the history of Israelite religion in many publications; see especially "Archaeology Confronts Biblical Criticism," *The American Scholar* 7 (1938): 176–88. His critiques of Wellhausen
are sprinkled in sections of several books, including *The Archaeology of Palestine and the Bible*
(New York: Fleming H. Revell Co., 1932); *From the Stone Age to Christianity* (Baltimore: Johns
Hopkins University Press, 1940); *Yahweh and the Gods of Canaan* (New York: Doubleday,
1968). For Albright's staunchly held view of the biblical prophets, see "The Archaeological
Background of the Hebrew Prophets of the Eighth Century," *Journal of Bible and Religion* 8
(1940): 135; his exalted opinion of Mosaism as the standard to which later prophets preached
reconversion was implicit in one of his first sweeping articles, "Archaeological Discovery in the
Holy Land," *BS* 79 (1922): 409. Note Matthews's strongly worded criticism of Albright's defense
of Mosaism in a review of *From the Stone Age*, published in the *Crozer Quarterly* 18 (1941):
246–49. McClellan published an essay on *Stone Age* that was entirely sympathetic to Albright's
historical, philosophical, and theological commitments in *Theological Studies* 2 (1942): 109–36.

was trained in the German tradition of Bible and Semitics—to Albright he embodied the end of the Wellhausenian era.[67] Pfeiffer had only very limited experience in field archaeology, however, and perhaps for this reason was more wary than Albright of claims made for the direct relevance of archaeology to understanding the Bible. Consequently, when he wrote his *Introduction to the Old Testament*,[68] published just after Albright's equally commanding *From the Stone Age to Christianity*, Pfeiffer made little reference to those discoveries that most likely would have exemplified the "archaeological phase" in Albright's first Gettysburg lecture and which he so skillfully used in *Stone Age*. This decision handed Albright the perfect symbol.

In Albright's published review of Pfeiffer's *Introduction*, the book seems to be both a text "out there" which other people may read, and a paradigmatic cipher in the framing perspective through which Albright mapped the territory of biblical studies for his own readers.[69] Although a "monumental" and "important landmark," Albright wrote, the work marked "the end of an era." Since it belonged to the passing epoch, it did not draw on "the new linguistic data or new philological techniques, thanks to which our approach to problems of Hebrew linguistic and literary history has been revolutionized in the past few years."

Indeed, Albright took the book as something to be corrected and updated, even praised faintly, while simultaneously defining it as a negativized antagonist to "our approach." Adopting the tone of one who was firmly positioned in the vanguard of the new era, Albright measured Pfeiffer's work unproblematically "in the light of recent progress," implying that the *Introduction* in the main was mired in stagnation. Seeding the review with various compliments and noting certain points of agreement, Albright nevertheless reserved his passion for courteous but forthright indictment. Pfeiffer was "surprisingly uninfluenced by the archaeological discoveries of the past two decades," and (invoking the mythic parent of such deficiency) fell again and again "under Wellhausenist influence." In a variety of ways readers of the review were told that Pfeiffer was uninformed or out of date.

67. Born in Italy, Pfeiffer studied in Berlin and Tübingen, and took his divinity degree with the Protestant faculty in Geneva. He received a Ph.D. from Harvard in 1922 and a master of theology the following year. He taught Bible and Semitic languages at Harvard and Boston University, was made curator of the Semitic Museum in 1931, and directed the Harvard-Baghdad School excavations at Nuzi in modern-day Iraq during 1928–29. See *Directory of American Scholars*, 3d ed. (New York: R. R. Bowker, 1957), 585.
68. Cambridge, Mass.: Harvard University Press, 1941.
69. The review appeared in *Journal of Biblical Literature* 61 (1942): 111–26.

In a letter to Pfeiffer, however, Albright put his opinion a bit more delicately. "The mass of material and the bibliography and indices will be invaluable," he wrote. "Of course, I do think it is the last of the 1880–1941 type of Introduction, since epigraphic discoveries are revolutionizing the entire field with unexampled rapidity, in spite of the war."[70] He was more candid with W. S. Ferguson, dean of Harvard's faculty of the humanities, in sentencing the book (and Pfeiffer) to an afterlife of antiquarian curiosity. The *Introduction* would "retain its importance for many years as a summation of the historical criticism of biblical literature up to the close of this phase of O.T. research." Citing examples of recently published inscriptions, Albright added, "To one familiar with the discoveries of recent decades, there is thus something strangely unreal about the entire book." And yet—here Albright seemed to suggest in Pfeiffer a perverse resistance to instruction— the "omission of all this material is deliberate, not in any way the result of ignorance."[71]

Pfeiffer responded to the published review with generosity and deference. Yet, he firmly attributed the absence of archaeological references in his book to a considered decision about a debatable point. He was skeptical of the claims made for the relevance of such finds to interpreting the Bible. "I agree with Woolley," he wrote, "when he said that the Bible contributes more to the interpretation of archaeological finds than vice versa." The cache of letters found at Lachish, a site not far from Jerusalem, were a case in point. "I am familiar with your brilliant interpretation of these difficult texts and I would utilize it were I writing a Hebrew dictionary or a Biblical commentary; but I find nothing in them of basic significance for a presentation of Jeremiah's times, life, and religious thought."[72]

There the matter stood: Pfeiffer held back and refused to embrace the substance of the "progress" that Albright so fervently encoded in his reformist reading of the rise of modern archaeology; Albright just as tenaciously dismissed such refusal, with the added suggestion that the objectivities of "science" demanded no other conclusion than the one he himself had drawn. One might say that the "renaissance" with which Albright identified had swept away Pfeiffer, and in its place were prophet-reformer Albright's new truths about the Bible.

70. Albright to Robert Pfeiffer, December 14, 1941.
71. Albright to William S. Ferguson, November 29, 1941. Ferguson had asked Albright for an evaluation of Pfeiffer's qualifications for election to the American Philosophical Society.
72. Robert Pfeiffer to Albright, July 2, 1942.

In his Gettysburg lecture, Albright also associated William A. Irwin with the passing era of Wellhausenian literary approaches. In some ways he seemed an even more potent symbol than Pfeiffer. Not only was Irwin tainted with theological liberalism and a socioanthropological approach to the Bible, both of which Albright viewed as characteristic of the University of Chicago, he belonged to a line of intellectual succession that was not at all rooted in the traditions of German philology as these had been imparted to Albright by Paul Haupt, his own teacher at Johns Hopkins.

A graduate of the University of Toronto, Irwin had studied at the University of Chicago under John Merlin Powis Smith, a pupil and then close associate of William Rainey Harper, the Yale-trained scholar who had served as the university's first president.[73] From Smith, Irwin received thorough schooling in Wellhausenian historical criticism of the Bible. In 1930, succeeding his teacher at the divinity school and Oriental Institute, Irwin extended Smith's deep interest in intellectual and social history, and worked within a faculty that was, on the whole, removed from, although not ignorant of, the field activities of biblical archaeologists. Since most archaeologists at the time were connected with old-line institutions in the Mid-Atlantic and New England states,[74] factional rivalry, or at least the perception that the youthful Midwest was resolutely independent of the East Coast centers of biblical scholarship, seemed a part of Irwin's and Albright's uneasy relationship.[75]

73. Richard Storr, *Harper's University: The Beginnings; A History of the University of Chicago* (Chicago: University of Chicago Press, 1966). See James Wind, *The Bible and the University: The Messianic Vision of William Rainey Harper* (Atlanta: Scholars Press, 1987).

74. The University of Chicago was an early corporate supporter of the American Schools of Oriental Research, and J. H. Breasted, the renowned Egyptologist from the Oriental Institute at Chicago, served as trustee of ASOR from 1926 to 1935. Yet for many years the management of the schools was primarily in the hands of a committee whose members rarely came from any school outside the eastern United States. Moreover, the chairs of the committee from 1902 to 1921 were all Easterners, and with reorganization of ASOR in 1921, two men, James Montgomery (University of Pennsylvania) and Millar Burrows (Yale University) served lengthy terms as president. It was not until 1949 that a scholar from the University of Chicago, Karl Kraeling, was chosen to lead ASOR. Irwin's only official contact with the world of biblical archaeology, and then only indirectly, was in 1934 when he served as a representative of the Oriental Institute at the Megiddo excavations in Palestine. For a sketch of Irwin's career, see the *National Cyclopedia of American Biography*, vol. 53 (New York: White, 1971), 213–14.

75. In 1891 a regional section of the national Society of Biblical Literature and Exegesis (SBLE) was established in Chicago; in late fall the following year, members decided, in the words of Harold Willoughby, a Chicagoan, to reorganize themselves, "in typically independent midwestern fashion," as the Chicago Society for Biblical Research, completely independent of the SBLE. Although open to guests from other regions of the country, and indeed the world, the new Society's proceedings were controlled by scholars based in the Midwest. See Harold R. Willoughby, ed., *The Study of the Bible Today and Tomorrow* (Chicago: University of Chicago

In 1939, a discussion involving the rejection of Irwin's paper on the marriage of Hosea (Hosea 1–3) by editors of the *Journal of Biblical Literature* (Albright's opinion was decisive in the matter) allowed such perceptions to surface in acrimonious debate. Professing to speak for many of his Chicago colleagues, Irwin raised the specter of political exclusion.[76] Albright, chair of the journal's editorial board, and Erwin Goodenough, chief editor, both vigorously denied the charge. However, in private Albright tossed a vague accusation back toward Chicago, saying that he and several of his younger colleagues (he probably meant his own former students) had had "the most incredible recent experiences and adventures with the Chicago organ, AJSL [*American Journal of Semitic Languages*], episodes that make Irwin's one experience with JBL [*Journal of Biblical Literature*] look pale by comparison."[77]

Of particular relevance to me is that, whatever is to be made of reputed factionalism, the episode brought forth Albright's judgments about Irwin's scholarly competence. These, I suggest, were not simply a matter of some objective standard of linguistic knowledge. His opinions seem also entwined with an ideological mapping of biblical scholarship and the values Albright ascribed to certain genealogies of professional training.

While claiming that Smith, Irwin's teacher, "did not have a spark of originality in him," Albright nonetheless respected him for his personal integrity and knowledge of Hebrew. He was dismayed, however, at Smith's slavish allegiance to the literary-historical, and "before archaeology," heritage of Wellhausen. Irwin, however, got no such indulgence. Implying that Irwin

---

Press, 1947), ix. This particular publication of the Society assessed the state of biblical studies in the postwar period, and even though Albright and Wright contributed to the volume, they in no sense dominated its perspective.

76. The paper dealt with sexual relations in Hosea and elsewhere in the Bible, and apparently was never published.

77. Albright to Erwin R. Goodenough, July 3, 1939. Irwin never published an article in the *Journal of Biblical Literature*, which for years had been managed by scholars in the East. Most of his work appeared in periodicals published by or closely associated with the University of Chicago, such as the *Journal of Religion* (successor to *Biblical World* [1893–1918] and *American Journal of Theology* [1897–1920]); *Journal of Bible and Religion*; *American Journal of Semitic Languages*, succeeded in 1942 by the *Journal of Near Eastern Studies*. See the bibliography of Irwin's works in Hobbs, *A Stubborn Faith* (Dallas: Southern Methodist University Press, 1956), 164–70. Irwin's and Albright's troubles never quite affected Ernest Wright. Located at McCormick Seminary in proximity to the University of Chicago scholars, Wright occasionally published essays in the Chicago journals. A bibliography may be found in Frank Moore Cross, Jr., et al., *Magnalia Dei. The Mighty Acts of God: Essays on the Bible and Archaeology in Memory of G. Ernest Wright* (Garden City, N.Y.: Doubleday, 1976), 579–93.

was a deficient mirror image of Smith, Albright simply dismissed Irwin, along with his colleague William Graham. "Neither is any scholar at all," Albright wrote to Goodenough. Although both men were of fine character and personal charm, Albright professed, Graham could not read German, and "[Irwin] knows very little Hebrew and little more about the modern literature." While friends described Irwin as a "grand person, with the heart of a child" (Albright himself said he "liked him personally"), Irwin's scholarship was "cheap and shoddy in the extreme, and the recent paper [submitted for review] is below his standard."[78]

Whatever Irwin's skills at Hebrew may have been (and of course private letters lend themselves to hyperbole), it is difficult to separate Albright's evaluation of the question from confessional and ideological, even personal, differences between the two men. Projected onto the symbolic landscape of Albright's reformist narrative, Irwin represented those faults and lapses characteristic of the passing "before archaeology" age. What was worse, Irwin failed to give Moses his due.

Although somewhat vaguely argued in *Stone Age*, Albright guarded the historical claim that Moses, even if anticipated by hints and tendencies among second-millennium peoples of the ancient Near East, was the first to articulate an exalted and truly monotheistic notion of God. In maintaining this view, Albright seemed to subscribe implicitly to a form of Christian dogma: the theological unity of revelation in the Old and New Testaments, or in Albright's historicized expression, Mosaic monotheism, even though expressed without the aid of Greek philosophical terminology, had to be consistent with much later Christian Trinitarian formulations.[79]

Irwin, as did many other scholars at the time, ascribed much less exalted features to early Israelite religion. In particular, Irwin reported his astonishment that Albright affirmed the "out of date" and "discredited" notion of

78. Albright to Goodenough, July 3, 1939.

79. See particularly Albright's summarizing statement in *Stone Age*, 271–72 (pagination refers to the Anchor Books edition [Garden City, N.Y.: Doubleday, 1957], the text of which was unchanged from the original 1940 publication). Albright's book occasioned much heated debate on the question of monotheism. Privately, Albright made clear the theological stake he held in a letter to H. H. Rowley. Commenting on Theophile Meek's opposition, he wrote, "We [Meek and I] can never agree on a definition of [Mosaic] monotheism, for the very simple reason that I refuse to accept a definition which denies monotheism to orthodox trinitarian Christianity." (Albright to H. H. Rowley, May 25, 1942.) At one point during the controversy, Albright took steps to assure that Ernest Wright had not publicly created a "conceivable breach in the line" on the issue. Albright to G. Ernest Wright, January 21, 1949; Wright to Albright, January 24, 1949; Albright to Wright, January 27, 1949.

Mosaic "primitive monotheism." Irwin went on to attack Albright the "dog-matician" for trying to maintain that such a grand intellectual and religious heritage had been preserved, essentially without historical development, through subsequent centuries.[80]

In the name of science and its claims to objective knowledge, Albright rejected studies of the Bible that were not firmly controlled by the presuppositions and derived data of archaeological research. Albright continually drew on such information to support his views about the antiquity and historical reliability of many biblical materials that others mistrusted, and to depict the history of biblical religion.[81] Irwin had had very little experience in field archaeology, and when he approached the Bible with similar claims to scientific objectivity, he worked with assumptions and interests of a literary-historical, not archaeologically focused, scholar. Thus, he investigated documentary sources of the Bible, editorial changes or additions to the biblical text, and—this was one of his major interests—reconstructed original forms of biblical poetry. The Bible itself, along with methods of historically oriented literary analysis, offered Irwin, respectively, his privileged object and paradigm for scientific study.[82] For Albright, biblical science meant mostly the study of the cultures to which the Bible pointed, through which it could be more accurately understood, and for which the excavated remains of long-disappeared cultures offered the main corrective to solipsistic literary analysis. Albright's scientific object was the Bible and biblical history explicated against their cultural environments.[83]

---

80. See W. A. Irwin's reviews of *Stone Age*, in *Journal of Religion* 21 (1941): 318–19; and *Christian Century* 58 (March 5, 1941): 322–23.

81. See his "Archaeology Confronts Biblical Criticism," *American Scholar* 7 (1938): 176–88.

82. Irwin's lecture, "Fifty Years of Old Testament Scholarship" (*Journal of Bible and Religion* 10 [1942]: 131–35, 183), delivered at the 50th anniversary meeting of the Chicago Society of Biblical Research, concentrated on literary studies of the Bible during the years 1891–1941. While extolling gains in understanding that had been made possible by archaeological finds, Irwin failed to mention many particulars or the contributions of Albright.

83. For example, see Irwin, "The Psalm of Habakkuk," *Journal of Near Eastern Studies* 1 (1942): 10–40. Albright haughtily dismissed Irwin's reconstruction of Habakkuk's psalm as "subjective," that is, uninformed by what Albright believed could be demonstrated about ancient biblical poetry from nonbiblical inscriptional evidence dug up by archaeologists. He pronounced that Irwin's reconstructed text "does not conform to any known Hebrew dialect or literary form." In Albright's opinion, he had developed the definitive line of investigation on the history of Semitic poetic form and style, and moreover, he applied, as he thought Irwin did not, the principles of classic philological analysis to the problems of biblical poetry. According to David Noel Freedman, Albright later wrote his own treatment of Habakkuk 3 partly to expose what he took to be Irwin's deficiencies. See Albright, "The Psalm of Habakkuk," in H. H. Rowley, ed., *Studies in Old Testament Prophecy* (Presented to Theodore H. Robinson;

I have drawn theoretical distinctions much sharper than they were in practice, of course, but I believe they approximately reflect Albright's often polemical and starkly polarized view. The difference in fundamental definition of what constituted proper biblical study helps account for Irwin's positive, and Albright's negative, valuation of Wellhausen. From the earliest days of his career, Albright had turned Julius Wellhausen into a negativized symbol of biblical study, and at about the time that Albright gave his Gettysburg lectures on Old Testament studies, Irwin wrote appreciatively of the importance of Wellhausen and made him into an emblem of the scientific literary approach to the Bible. Along the way, Irwin pointedly objected to what he saw as Albright's superficial dismissal of Wellhausen's supposed enslavement to "Hegelianism." Irwin went on to suggest how much of Wellhausen's legacy Albright accepted, while professing his distance from it.[84]

The differences between Albright and Irwin do not seem to have had much to do with their notions of science, or scientific knowledge. On these matters, they had a good deal in common. Both were convinced that scientific method, as applied to ancient literature and history, offered the only avenue to true understanding; they both assumed an objective grounding for their claims about the world, or as Irwin put it in his appreciation of Wellhausen, "the firm faith that the Universe is rational and that the reasoning powers of

---

Edinburgh: T. & T. Clark, 1950), 1–18. See also Albright, "The Earliest Forms of Hebrew Verse," *Journal of the Palestine Oriental Society* 2 [1922]: 69–86; "The Oracles of Balaam," *Journal of Biblical Literature* 63 (1944): 207–33. Albright also condemned Irwin's study of Ezekiel, in which Irwin sought a rigorous inductive method to discern the original core of Ezekiel's sayings now buried within a mass of later editorial addition (*The Problem of Ezekiel: An Inductive Approach* [Chicago: University of Chicago Press, 1943]). This was, in a way, a classic Wellhausenian analysis, but updated with attention to the supposed regularities of traditional style and literary genres. Albright called it "Priceless Piffle" and a *"Missgeburt"* (Wright to Albright, January 28, 1944; Albright to Wright, February 3, 1944). Somewhat later, Albright scornfully dismissed one sympathetic reviewer, I. G. Matthews, who had earlier severely criticized Albright's *Stone Age*, as "an old fool" because he had called Irwin's book "the threshold of a new appreciation of the book of Ezekiel" (Albright to Wright, April 7, 1944; see the review in *Crozer Quarterly* 21 [1944]: 182–83; see also I. G. Matthews, *Ezekiel* [Philadelphia: American Baptist Publication Society, 1939]). Irwin's book received other positive reviews (e.g., by W. R. Taylor, Irwin's former colleague at the University of Toronto, in the *Journal of Religion* 24 [1944]: 289; unsigned, in *Christian Century* 61 [April 26, 1944]: 530). However, the book was never reviewed in the *Journal of Biblical Literature*. If Albright is to be taken at face value—he was then book review editor of the *Journal*—he had been turned down by the "four best men in the east" and he was unwilling to "expose a young scholar to what he would incur by courting Irwin's hostility" (Albright to Wright, February 3, 1944).

84. "The Significance of Julius Wellhausen," *Journal of Bible and Religion* 12 (1944): 160–73. Privately, Albright branded the article as "silly" (Albright to Wright, August 5, 1944).

the human mind are adequate to some dependable understanding of it."[85]
Both studied the Bible if not directly as a theological enterprise, then at least
as a way of furthering the interests of Christian theology and practice.[86]

Yet, for Irwin, Wellhausen stood for highly valued scientific study that is
centered on *text as writing*, that is, a kind of textual analysis that is "throughout an appeal to objective evidence: an analysis of literary and historical
sources and the employment of these in that logically objective way which
we associate with the historic method."[87] As mentioned, Albright charged
Wellhausen with negative significance. He represented biblical criticism that
was outmoded, speculative, and excessively subjective, unchecked by empirical facts and control that Albright was convinced archaeology offered. New,
reliable, truly scientific biblical study meant the "backgrounds approach," a
study of the world *around* the Bible so as to understand better the world *in*
the Bible.

Differing symbolic roles given to Wellhausen, opposed though not ex-
clusive paradigms of biblical study, all within shared discourse of historical
science, led inevitably to tensions. I do not mean simply personal dislikes
but, rather, contests over formations of social power, in which ideological
commitments emerge. Efforts to supplant or defend Wellhausen offer one
example. Another, which similarly surfaced between Albright and Irwin,
involved graduate students.

As mentioned earlier, Albright had been pleased enough with the students gathered around him in the mid-1940s that he was no longer worried
whether his views on the Bible would win out. Yet Albright once confided
that he suspected Irwin's harmful influence was preventing Allan Wehrli,
another of Albright's students, from finishing his dissertation. Noting that
Irwin had delivered four lectures at Eden Theological Seminary where
Wehrli was then teaching, Albright wrote, "Knowing more than I care to

85. "Julius Wellhausen," 171.
86. See, above all, *From the Stone Age* (in the preface to the German translation, Albright
expressed the hope that he could "deliver a small contribution to Christian theology of the
future" [*Von der Steinzeit zum Christentum* (Bern: Francke, 1949)], 7); *Archaeology and the
Religion of Israel*. See W. A. Irwin, "Revelation in the Old Testament," in Harold R. Willoughby,
ed., *The Study of the Bible Today and Tomorrow* (Chicago: University of Chicago Press, 1947),
247–67.
87. "Julius Wellhausen," 164. Irwin's book *Ezekiel* well exemplifies his approach. He took
great care to arrive at what to him were objective literary and stylistic criteria with which to
discriminate original from spurious material in the biblical book; yet in the spirit of scientific
inquiry, he claimed no finality for his results, and remained open to further consideration of the
argument and the evidence on which it was based (pp. vii–xi).

know about Irwin's methods, I can see that someone has 'plowed with my heifer.' Luckily there are not many Irwins about, but they can do a lot of harm with their underhanded methods."[88] A few years later, after a lecture tour of the Midwest, Albright remarked that he found another scholar, Arnold Rhodes of the Louisville Theological Seminary, to be "very earnest, still too much influenced by Irwin, but by no means sold on Chicago and willing to learn from Baltimore."[89]

I have constructed this picture of Albright's authorizing narrative and paradigmatic figures in fundamentally hermeneutical terms as one way of imagining Albright the scholar, and the world of ideological commitments and values which he transmitted to his sons and they to his grandsons. Even allowing for differences in nuance among members of subsequent generations, the main picture I believe accurately reflects the general social situation of competing interpretive assumptions, values, and commitments played out as ideological struggle over right and wrong, old and new, competence and incompetence, reputation and influence. Within the paradigms of science, Albright and, insofar as they followed him, his students, may be understood as enacting a myth of hermeneutical reform and supplantation. They appealed to the authority of the Enlightenment and its scientific legacy, then to the power of the new science of archaeology, and finally to Albright himself, to displace what they depicted as simple, objective inadequacies of those they opposed.

To the Albrightean generation fell the duty to overturn certain of the effects of Wellhausen in these postwar days. The new warriors were called to recover the truth of the Bible obscured and dulled by a tradition of outmoded

88. Albright to Jacob Myers, June 15, 1943. Irwin's lectures at Eden were entitled: "The Relevance of the Old Testament for Today"; "The Old Testament Conception of History"; "The Old Testament and National Vitality"; "The Vision of God in the Old Testament." (Archives, Eden Theological Seminary, St. Louis, Missouri.) Almost a year later, the suspicion (was it also a kind of anxiety?) had not in the least subsided: "Since Irwin gave some lectures at Eden Seminary," Albright wrote, "Wehrli won't answer any of my letters, so you can see that Irwin must have told him some cock-and-bull story to poison the well." (Albright to Wright, March 17, 1944.) According to Wehrli's son, who is now the president of Eden Seminary, before coming to Albright, Allan Wehrli had studied with J. M. P. Smith at the University of Chicago. In contrast to many of Albright's graduate students who had been sent to Johns Hopkins by Albright's students of an earlier generation, Wehrli's intellectual pedigree may have seemed suspect to Albright from the beginning.

89. Albright to Freedman, August 8, 1950. Born in 1913, Arnold Rhodes received theological degrees from the Louisville Seminary, where he taught from 1944 until his retirement in 1983. He earned a Th.D. from Southern Baptist Theological Seminary in 1947 and three years later received his Ph.D. from the University of Chicago.

interpretation, to reconfigure the methods of biblical study, and, hence, to place knowledge about the Bible on what was to them a firmer footing of archaeological and linguistic science. These new tools reaffirmed to Albright and his sons in these postwar years the historical reliability of much that had been dismissed from the Bible by those belonging to the older generation, and—this was true especially for Ernest Wright—fostered renewed appreciation of the Scriptures as a contemporary theological resource for Christian churches.

When projected against this implicit canvas of the two ages, the question of membership in the planned Biblical Colloquium, especially in the light of Wright's ambitions, was not a trivial matter. A person's competence considered abstractly perhaps seemed less important than gathering together a group of people with a particularly formed *Albrightean* competence who could be useful—in Howie's case with some help—in the battle to establish truth triumphant. It seems the Colloquium might have advanced, as Albright said in the Gettysburg lectures, the "renaissance of our day."

Planting and Reaping

Even in his absence, Albright seemed to dominate the first meeting of the Colloquium. On Albright's advice, Howie was, despite doubts, invited to participate. The Bright-Howie collaborative project, and Albright himself, apparently were discussed by all those first participants. Afterward, Umhau Wolf could hardly contain his excitement. "We had a wonderful time, putting you together, trying to interpret you and re-interpret you," he wrote to Albright.[90] The group had made plans, too, following Freedman's lead, for reprinting and disseminating Albright's work. Wolf was certain that Albright would have already heard about this from the "men more closely connected to you than I am, since they had more time with you than my one short year. . . . I am flattered to be in with that group. . . . I believe we have some wonderful plans if we can bring them to pass. Your encouragement and leadership is important, of course."

Ernest Wright also reported to his teacher. The "Albright gang" was enthusiastic to say the least, "sparked by Cross and Freedman, and they have big ideas of what they might do."[91] Four seize-the-future reports were

90. Carl Umhau Wolf to Albright, December 5, 1950.
91. Wright to Albright, December 20, 1950.

given: Wright on "Needed Projects and Work to Be Done in O.T. Field"; Cross, "Concerning the Projected Cross-Wright *Introduction to the Old Testament*"; Freedman, "A New Hebrew Grammar, and Plans for Publication of Brief Monographs"; Bright, "The Bright-Howie Proposed *History of Israel*."[92] Freedman recalled that the group extensively discussed Wright's then-dormant plan for a theological dictionary. Wright even assigned studies of Hebrew words during that first meeting, some of which were to be presented at subsequent gatherings of the Colloquium.[93]

One of the "big ideas"—it was apparently mostly Freedman's idea—was that the seminar should embark on an ambitious plan to reprint Albright's books and distribute them as widely as possible. Even before the Colloquium met, Freedman had been involved in the repackaging and sale of Albright's *The Biblical Period from Abraham to Ezra*.[94] Now, he zealously pursued an expanded goal, partly to subsidize meetings and other publications envisioned by the Colloquium, and partly to assure that whole new generations of students, potential converts to the Albrightean way, would have easy access to Albright's work.

Freedman wanted to reprint *The Biblical Period* a second time, and after the meeting in Pittsburgh he wrote to Albright, "I am determined to distribute 10,000 copies before we are done. At least 5,000 anyway."[95] Albright secured permission from a reluctant holder of the copyright (the material had already appeared in two formats, and just a year earlier), advanced initial capital, and paid for three hundred copies himself.[96] This proved by far the most successful venture of the Colloquium in its early days. Perhaps unaware that Albright had urged that he be excluded from membership in the Colloquium, Herbert May celebrated the book's appearance in the

92. Personal Notebook of the Biblical Colloquium, G. Ernest Wright. Courtesy of Emily (Mrs. G. Ernest) Wright, Lexington, Mass.

93. Memorial Minute for G. Ernest Wright. *Minutes*, Biblical Colloquium, November 1974. The plan for a theological dictionary had been developed with Westminster Press a few years earlier, but differences among Wright, Albright, and the Press led all parties to halt planning in 1946. Wright, however, continued to seek ways to produce the reference work since he believed it to be "the most important single project in the O.T. field" he knew of at the time. (Wright to Albright, January 6, 1947.) A student at Harvard from the early 1960s reported that Wright regularly assigned dictionary articles to selected graduate students. See Chapter 3 below, "Not Words Alone."

94. New York: Harper & Brothers, 1949; the book was an expansion and revision of Albright's essay in Louis Finkelstein, ed., *The Jews: Their History, Culture, and Religion* (New York: Harper & Brothers, 1949).

95. Freedman to Albright, December 8, 1950.

96. Freedman to Ruth Norton (Mrs. William Foxwell) Albright, March 5, 1951.

Journal of Biblical Literature, and even noted that volume discounts were available for classroom use.[97] By the fall of 1957, *The Biblical Period* would sell 16,000 copies, far beyond Freedman's most ambitious hopes.[98]

The achievement was remarkable considering that during these years the world of biblical scholars was quite small and mainly oriented around colleges and universities in the eastern half of America. Although doubling in the postwar decades, membership in the Society of Biblical Literature and Exegesis stood at about one thousand in 1950. Campus facilities could easily accommodate the several hundred who attended annual meetings, and the gatherings, though changing, still resembled the congenial exchanges of an "amplified faculty club."[99]

The Colloquium quickly reissued two other Albright works: *The Bible After Twenty Years*[100] and a considerably older survey, *Recent Discoveries in Bible Lands*.[101] While Freedman worked closely with Doubleday to bring out an updated version of *From the Stone Age to Christianity*,[102] he also discussed with Harper's the possibility of publishing a single-volume edition of *The Biblical Period* and *The Bible After Twenty Years*, along with other shorter works. The advantages, as Freedman pointed out to Albright, were significant mass circulation far beyond the capabilities of the Albrightean network, and increased royalty payments to the Colloquium.[103] A few months later, at Wright's urging, members of the Colloquium planned an anthology of Albright's previously published essays. Wright even proposed that one of his own books on biblical theology be reprinted as a companion piece to Albright's *Biblical Period*.[104]

97. *Journal of Biblical Literature* 70 (1951): 175.

98. Freedman to Albright, October 3, 1957. While this first publishing venture was underway, Freedman approached Albright about distributing reprints of his survey of ancient Near Eastern history, then in preparation for *The Interpreter's Bible*, George Buttrick et al., eds. (New York: Abingdon-Cokesbury, 1951–57). The reprint was never published. Freedman to Albright, Nov. 11, 1950; Albright to Freedman, December 3, 1950.

99. Ernest Saunders, *Searching the Scriptures. A History of the Society of Biblical Literature, 1880–1980* (Chico, Calif.: Scholars Press, 1982), 41, 46.

100. Pittsburgh: The Biblical Colloquium, 1954. Reprinted from *Religion in Life* 21 (1952).

101. Pittsburgh: The Biblical Colloquium, 1955. Originally published in 1936 by Funk and Wagnalls, New York. By late November of 1956, the Colloquium had sold about 2,000 copies each of *Recent Discoveries* and *The Bible After Twenty Years*. (Freedman to Albright, Oct. 10, 1956.)

102. Freedman to Albright, November 11, 1956. The book appeared in 1957.

103. Freedman to Albright, September 16, 1956.

104. Wright to Freedman, June 22, 1957, CDNF. Wright had in mind reprinting his half of a coauthored work: G. Ernest Wright and Reginald Fuller, *The Book of the Acts of God* (Garden City, N.Y.: Doubleday, 1957). This book was never reprinted, but by 1961 Wright had secured

The Biblical Colloquium expended similar energies on behalf of its founding members too. It subsidized publication of Cross and Freedman's *Early Hebrew Orthography*.[105] Originating as the first of two jointly written Ph.D. theses under Albright, the book extended and solidified the base of Albright's pioneering work in orthographic analysis. Cross and Freedman wrote of the enlarged fund of inscriptional material that made necessary a "complete transformation of older ideas regarding the history of orthographic developments" in the ancient Near East. Hidden in their prose was an echo of Albright's myth of supplantation, with its vanquished Wellhausen. "No longer must the scholar depend upon a few hints from partly misunderstood inscriptions," they wrote. No longer need one "develop his views with the aid of subjectively derived principles of evolution." Rather, there can now be a "solid basis" for describing the "fundamental laws governing the history and practice" of orthography.[106] This book not only embodied the Albrightean myth, it set forth the basis on which Albright had applied these same principles of historical orthography to reconstructing and dating biblical poetry.[107]

George Mendenhall's *Law and Covenant* was first presented at a meeting of the Colloquium in 1953.[108] A year later it appeared in *Biblical Archaeologist*,[109] a journal that had been founded in 1938 by Wright with counsel and involvement of Albright.[110] The following year, the Colloquium

---

a publisher for the anthology of Albright's articles, and was working out details of the project. (Wright to Freedman, December 8, 1961, CDNF.)

105. Published by the American Oriental Society, New Haven, 1952. Freedman to Frank Moore Cross, Jr., February 3, 1957, CDNF.

106. *Hebrew Orthography*, 7.

107. Albright, "The Earliest Forms of Hebrew Verse," *Journal of the Palestine Oriental Society* 2 (1922): 69–86; "The Song of Deborah in the Light of Archaeology," *BASOR* 62 (1936): 26–31; "The Oracles of Balaam," *Journal of Biblical Literature* 63 (1944): 207–33; "The Psalm of Habakkuk," in H. H. Rowley, ed., *Studies in Old Testament Prophecy* (Edinburgh: Clark, 1950), 1–18. Cross and Freedman would continue this version of Albright's "backgrounds approach" in a number of essays drawn from the second of their jointly written dissertations: Frank Moore Cross and David Noel Freedman, "The Blessing of Moses," *Journal of Biblical Literature* 67 (1948): 191–210; "The Song of Miriam," *Journal of Near Eastern Studies* 14 (1955): 237–50. Much later, this second dissertation was published intact as *Studies in Yahwistic Poetry* (Missoula, Mont.: Scholars Press, 1975). See also David Noel Freedman, *Pottery, Poetry, and Prophecy* (Winona Lake, Ind.: Eisenbrauns, 1980).

108. Personal Notebook of the Biblical Colloquium, G. Ernest Wright.

109. *Biblical Archaeologist* 17 (1954): 26–46, 50–76. The essay was printed yet another time by the Albrightean circle in Edward F. Campbell, Jr., and David Noel Freedman, eds., *Biblical Archaeologist Reader 3* (Garden City, N.Y.: Doubleday, 1970), 3–53.

110. See exchanges between Wright and Albright, November 15, 1937, and December 1, 1937; January 21, 1940; May 8, 1940; September 1 and 3, 1940.

Fig. 6.   George Mendenhall (right) and his foreman, Salin Qureyshi, Jericho excavation, 1956. Courtesy of George E. Mendenhall.

reprinted it.[111] Innovative in his use of ancient Near Eastern materials, Mendenhall offered particular dress for a number of unshakable Albrightean convictions: the antiquity of the Mosaic tradition, the primacy of Moses in the history of Israelite religion, and the theological purity of Moses' religion.[112] A Harvard student recalled that as late as the early 1970s Mendenhall's book was a "centerpiece" of Humanities 100, "Introduction to Biblical Studies," because it was still taken, despite substantive criticism, to bolster confidence in the Bible's presentation of the Mosaic exodus and Sinai materials.[113] Mendenhall did not simply credit Moses with formulating the singular truth of genuine monotheism, as was Albright's claim, but he sought to give Moses'

111. Pittsburgh: The Biblical Colloquium, 1955. Within a year it had sold about 2,000 copies. Freedman to Albright, October 10, 1956.

112. The mature statement appears in Albright's *From the Stone Age to Christianity*. Some of the themes had been adumbrated eighteen years earlier in "Archaeological Discovery in the Holy Land," *BS* 79 (1922): 401–17.

113. Interview, 1994. For the substantive criticism, see Dennis J. McCarthy, S.J., *Treaty and Covenant* (Analecta Biblica 21; Rome: Pontifical Biblical Institute, 1963; 2d rev. and enlarged ed., 1978).

innovation a more specific theological content and set it firmly (and early) against ancient Near Eastern conventions: one God, one covenant with Israel (conceived as a prestate historical unity in terms of second-millennium conventions of treaty making), and one genuinely Mosaic covenantal law, the Ten Commandments.

Mendenhall also sought to further Albright's attempts to counter the influence of Julius Wellhausen's picture of ancient Israelite religion. Albright did not object to Wellhausen's theory of multiple documents in the Bible— in fact he accepted this principle as a condition of all his own historical work. But he scorned Wellhausen's developmental history of ancient Israel's religion insofar as it denied Moses and his monotheism their rightful place in antiquity or, in short, contravened Albright's religious commitments.

At the 1956 meeting of the Biblical Colloquium, Mendenhall took up the campaign. He hesitated before going beyond the inner circle, however, and so asked Albright to review what he described as a "rather ambitious attempt at drawing up a more adequate hypothesis on the History of Israelite Religion to replace Wellhausen. . . . The boys [at the Colloquium] were very enthusiastic about it," he wrote, adding that "Freedman is planning to publish the first half of the paper . . . in the March issue of JBL [*Journal of Biblical Literature*], and I am incorporating a considerable number of your statements included in FSAC [*From the Stone Age to Christianity*]."[114]

By 1956, such successes at disseminating their views as the Albrightean sons were enjoying encouraged Freedman to recommend that Doubleday, with the cooperation of the Colloquium, publish some German and Scandinavian works in English translation. As usual, Freedman consulted Albright; he mentioned a collection of essays by Albrecht Alt.[115]

Albright had known Alt since 1921. They met in Jerusalem when Alt directed the German School—Albright heard him preach and received him for tea a few days later.[116] The young Albright wrote that he was a "splendid scholar and a charming man, one of the best preachers I have ever heard."[117]

---

114. George Mendenhall to Albright, November 28, 1956. By the time Mendenhall wrote to Albright, *Stone Age* had become a major force in the field. It had appeared in a second edition (1946) and had been translated into German (1949), French (1951), and Hebrew (1953), each time with revisions and updated notes. Wright recorded Mendenhall's lecture as "A New Hypothesis Concerning the History of Israel." The plan to publish the piece in the *Journal of Biblical Literature* did not materialize, at least not right away.

115. Freedman to Albright, July 13, 1956. The essays in question had appeared in Albrecht Alt, *Kleine Schriften zur Geschichte des Volkes Israels I* (Munich: C. H. Beck'sche, 1953).

116. Albright, "Diary," December 11 and 22, 1921.

117. Albright to his mother, January 22, 1922.

They corresponded in subsequent years, and in 1929, Albright praised Alt's study "God of the Fathers" as something "worth reading" and marking "a new step forward in our knowledge of the early religion of Israel."[118] Nearly thirty years later, Albright was more cautious. By then, one of Alt's most prominent students, Martin Noth, was known for distinctly non-Albrightean attitudes: skepticism toward the historical reliability of the Bible's earliest materials and doubts that archaeological finds could contribute much toward understanding these literary traditions.[119]

Thus, when Freedman proposed translating some of Alt's essays, Albright moved quickly to dampen enthusiasm. He advised against translation, saying it would be costly and "probably inaccurate at best." Better to concentrate on the publications of the Biblical Colloquium so as not to dilute them "until they have no meaning." There still was a "yawning gap" between the Albrightean approach and that of European scholars. Besides, Albright added, he did not think that Freedman could take on any more editorial activities without affecting his own productivity and health.[120]

Cautionary flags stood at the opening and closing of Albright's statement. He expressed concern about costs and accuracy, an odd reservation for a scholar who knew many languages and translated all manner of textual material; at the close, he worried about Freedman's health and productivity. Nested in the middle was a quite different issue: ideological divisions, a "yawning gap" among critics of the Bible, with the added suggestion that efforts to create a certain Albrightean dominance in North American scholarship, and a preference for the archaeological backgrounds approach to the Bible, might be weakened.

It was not a new concern. Earlier, it will be recalled, when Cross, Freedman, and Mendenhall were studying with him, Albright had written about the brilliant students who would help his "views about the Bible win out."[121] Soon thereafter, Albright advised Ernest Wright—at the time Wright was

118. Albright to Julian Morgenstern, November 24, 1929. Morgenstern Papers, American Jewish Archives, Cincinnati. The essay by Alt was *Der Gott der Väter* (Beiträge zur Wissenschaft vom Alten und Neuen Testament, 3d series, vol. 12 [Stuttgart: Kohlhammer, 1929]). See the translation by R. A. Wilson, in Albrecht Alt, *Essays on Old Testament History and Religion* (Oxford: Blackwell, 1966), 1–77.

119. See, for example, M. Noth, *Überlieferungsgeschichte des Pentateuch* (Stuttgart: Kohlhammer, 1948), or *A History of the Pentateuchal Traditions*, trans. Bernhard Anderson (Englewood Cliffs, N.J.: Prentice-Hall, 1972). See also Noth's *Geschichte Israels* (Göttingen: Vandenhoeck & Ruprecht, 1950). The 2d edition (1954) was translated as *The History of Israel* (New York: Harper & Row, 1960).

120. Albright to Freedman, July 17, 1956.

121. Albright to parents, December 22, 1946.

involved in plans for a new series of books on biblical theology—to give preference to Americans, that is, Albrighteans. Get George Mendenhall to submit his monograph on the Hebraic idea of taking vengeance (*nqm*), Albright wrote. Publishing this material would be more valuable than merely translating the theological studies of Walther Eichrodt, whom Albright and Wright nonetheless admired. Why? Because Mendenhall "marks out new lines of thought and is strictly American in genesis and execution."[122]

Similar rivalries came to the surface in the circumstances surrounding John Bright's *A History of Israel*.[123] Announced to the Biblical Colloquium in 1950 as a joint effort with Carl Howie, it eventually became exclusively Bright's project when Howie left academic life. In 1954 Bright presented the seminar with a prelude to this work, an essay entitled "Prolegomena to History, Especially the Alt School."[124] This first effort grew into a modestly, but forthrightly, stated defense of Albright's approach to the traditions of early Israel.

In effect, the Colloquium vetted the substance of a monograph that Bright would later publish as *Early Israel in Recent History Writing*.[125] Appealing to his and Albright's authority, Wright gave the little book its imprimatur, and urged that it be published in Studies in Biblical Theology, a series he had helped establish.

> My feeling about it is well summed up by W. F. Albright, who has also read the MS and who writes: "I have just returned a carbon copy of John Bright's remarkable monograph . . . ; it is a brilliant piece of work—a true tour de force. I could think of no change or addition which would not weaken its force and complicate matters unnecessarily. I hope that it can be published speedily."[126]

122. Albright to Wright, May 19, 1949, in reply to Wright's letter, May 17, 1949. See George Mendenhall, "God of Vengeance, Shine Forth!" *Wittenberg Bulletin* 45 (1948): 37–42. The new series, Studies in Biblical Theology (London: SCM Press), did not turn out to be as restricted as Albright may have hoped. Indeed, the series early on included Eichrodt's *Man in the Old Testament*, trans. K. and R. Gregor Smith (London: SCM Press, 1951). In any case, Albright seems to have preferred Eichrodt's theological commitments over those of most other European scholars at the time. Earlier, in 1944, he had even suggested that Eichrodt's theology volumes would make a good basis for a dictionary of Hebrew theological terms. See below, Chapter 3, "Not Words Alone."

123. Philadelphia: Westminster Press, 1959.

124. Wright, Personal Notebook. See Freedman to Albright, July 11, 1955.

125. *Early Israel in Recent History Writing: A Study in Method* (Studies in Biblical Theology 19 [London: SCM Press, 1956]).

126. Ernest Wright to R. Gregor Smith, July 20, 1955. Copy courtesy Charles Bright.

Bright's monograph was something of a manifesto by the "Baltimore school" against what Bright called the "Alt-Noth" school. Following their teacher, the Albrighteans presumed that reliable history could be gotten from the narratives of exodus, wilderness wanderings, and entry into the land of Canaan; Alt and his student Noth treated these same biblical materials as national and popular tradition, a subset of folklore, and in the absence of confirming evidence were very skeptical as to their historical worth. The Baltimore school was greatly vested in archaeology, and even though architectural remains and artifacts were largely mute traces of ancient life, they believed nevertheless that such physical traces could help evaluate these early biblical traditions, which were, in any case, presumed to be reliable until disproven by archaeology. Alt and Noth, though just as vested, gave the results of archaeological work far less a privileged position in reconstructing Israel's earliest history.

Some of Albright's students of these years, especially John Bright and Ernest Wright, joined their historical reconstructions to theology. They seemed to build as much on Albright's own proclivities as on their own,

Fig. 7.   John Bright when he was teaching at Union Theological Seminary, ca. 1950. Courtesy of Union Theological Seminary, Richmond, Virginia.

and may have been reacting against the prominent questioning by Rudolph Bultmann of the relevance of historical facticity to Christian theology.[127] In *Early Israel,* Bright made the join explicit. He asserted that Old Testament theology was concerned with real historical events and their interpretation through religious faith, and thus actual history could never be a matter of indifference to the theologian. Hence, for theological reasons, these sons of Albright needed to recover external history behind those narratives that spoke of Israelites' meeting God at discrete times and particular places. Otherwise, to them the religious claims, lacking firmly established historical grounding, would be suspect and insubstantial. Alt and Noth had made no commitment to such historicized biblical theology, and so were more free to refuse the historical quest when biblical tradition to them seemed folkloristic, and when artifacts from the ground were silent. By constructing the differences between himself (the Albrighteans) and the Alt-Noth school in terms of a series of sharp polarities, Bright thus made a bid in the name of science and archaeology to control the picture of ancient Israel's "past" as both reliable history and religious truth for Christian readers.

In time, Bright prepared *A History of Israel,* which turned out to be a kind of surrogate for Albright's voice, reverently presented.[128] Not only had members of the Colloquium discussed the work in its early stages, but Bright had asked Albright and Wright to review chapters of the *History* as well, clearly wanting above all to make the views of Albright widely accessible to students and pastors. On one occasion, referring to his treatment of the Israelite ancestors, Bright wrote, "I hope that what I have done will pass muster and will be no great discredit to the position (that is, your own position) which I have tried to represent."[129]

127. See Hans W. Bartsch, ed., *Kerygma und Mythos: Ein Theologische Gespräch* (Hamburg: Herbert Reich, 1948). Some of the material from a later edition, including Bultmann's manifesto, was translated by Reginald Fuller in Hans W. Bartsch, ed., *Kerygma and Myth: A Theological Debate* (New York: Macmillan, 1953). Albright repeatedly referred to his distaste for Bultmann's existentialist thought, and gathered together his objections in a review of Bultmann's *The Presence of Eternity: History and Eschatology* (Edinburgh: The University Press, 1957), published in *Journal of Biblical Literature* 77 (1958): 244–48. The book review was expanded and published in Albright, *History, Archaeology and Christian Humanism* (New York: McGraw-Hill, 1964), 272–84.

128. See the foreword of John Bright, *A History of Israel* (Philadelphia: Westminster Press, 1959), 10–11.

129. John Bright to Albright, April 30, 1956. See also letters of May 9, July 20 and 25, and November 5 of that same year. Also, Wright to Bright, May 24, 1958, copy courtesy of Charles Albright.

When the book was published, the Albrighteans praised it as a kind of flagship for the fleet. Ernest Wright told Bright that he had written a review for the Westminster *Bookman* to give the book "as good a send off as I know how to do." He hoped that before year's end, he could publish in *Biblical Archaeologist*, a journal that Wright edited, a more extensive review comparing Bright's *History* with a rival volume by Martin Noth, "to the detriment of Noth and to the credit of your book, and the biblical archaeologist!"[130] Dewey Beegle, who had taken a Ph.D. with Albright in 1952, wrote that the book "should consolidate the position of the 'Baltimore School.' "[131] Albright himself extolled the book as without comparison and "far superior" to Noth's *History*. "I shall mention your book on every possible occasion," he told Bright.[132]

The *History* seemed to handily expose and confirm that "yawning gap" which Albright had earlier mentioned in connection with translating some of Alt's essays. Writing to Freedman, Albright enthusiastically praised the book for its clear contrast to the "Alt-Noth school."[133] Yet, left obscure within this rhetorical polarity between Baltimore and Europe were the foundational choices and preferences, the ideological commitments, that helped frame the perspectives from which Albright and his students ordered the world of scholarship, settled the "facts" of biblical history, and even determined the truth about books *about* biblical history. Believing unproblematically in positivistic historical inquiry and its privileged position in yielding human-istic and theological truth, Albright could easily objectify reasons for the "yawning gap." In contrast to John Bright (and the Albrighteans), Alt and his pupils, though they started out well enough, had simply been deprived of empirical data during the war years, Albright wrote in a review essay about a year later. As a result—here he implied that the German scholars took a misguided turn toward subjectivity—they pursued research "along a priori lines," lost touch with "archaeological and philological fact . . . [and] were inclined to discount the evidence of archaeological stratigraphy and to close their eyes to linguistic arguments."[134] The Alt-Noth school doubted what Albright (and John Bright's *History*) held to be sure: "the

130. Wright to John Bright, September 10, 1959. Copy courtesy of Charles Bright.
131. Beegle to Albright, May 22, 1960.
132. Albright to John Bright, November 8, 1959. Courtesy of Charles Bright.
133. Albright to Freedman, November 15, 1959. See Albright to F. Charles Fensham, December 16, 1959.
134. *History, Archaeology, and Christian Humanism* (New York: McGraw-Hill, 1964), 265–67. Originally published as "Eric Voeglin: Order and History," *Theological Studies* 22 (1961): 270–79.

career of Moses and the subsequent Israelite occupation of Palestine are to be dated in the thirteenth century B.C. . . . It is no longer possible to separate early Israelite religion sharply from that of later Israel; explicit if nonphilosophical monotheism must go back to the age of Moses, and the other essential principles and institutions of Biblical religion also go back to Israelite beginnings."[135]

Since this self-designation of place against the "Alt-Noth school" as inscribed in Bright's *History* would most likely have been a part of Freedman's educational experience, the proposal in 1956 that the Colloquium publish translations of Alt's writings now seems somewhat surprising. It is understandable, however. At the time, John Bright had only just begun to codify Albrightean opposition to an "Alt-Noth school," and Albright himself may have been ambivalent—admiring of Alt and suspicious of Noth.[136] In any event, Freedman apparently submitted to Albright's wishes, as nothing came of the idea. Indeed, whether out of principle or pragmatic considerations, the Colloquium never published research outside the parameters set by the Baltimore school.

An Albrightean Bible

Albright's worry at the time that Freedman might be taking on too much editorial work was probably not disingenuous. About a year earlier, he had become editor of the *Journal of Biblical Literature*, and besides, his energies would now be required for the *Anchor Bible*, plans for which were already far advanced when Alt's writings were being discussed.[137] Nothing that had been accomplished in the six years since the Colloquium's founding would surpass this project in scope and ambition. And nothing would rival it as an opportunity for the sons and grandsons of Albright to shape the practice of biblical studies according to their convictions. It was assumed from the start that members of the Colloquium would provide the core of talent for the venture. Albright and Freedman were to be coeditors, but frequent consultations with Cross and Wright suggest that these four men

135. *History, Archaeology, and Christian Humanism*, 266–67.
136. Freedman reported much later that Albright once hailed Alt as a "second Wellhausen," to which Alt replied sternly that there was only one Wellhausen. Freedman to Burke O. Long, April 30, 1995.
137. Many years later Freedman reported that Western Seminary gave no relief to members of its faculty who took on major publishing activities. Freedman to Long, April 30, 1995.

constituted an unofficial editorial committee, at least in the early stages of planning. It was Freedman, however, who supplied much of the energy and organizational drive, and who, with Albright's concurrence, attended to most details of the project. More than anyone else, so far as the record allows me to judge, Freedman viewed the series strategically, as an extension of what the Biblical Colloquium could accomplish in setting the unified results of an Albrightean approach before generations of Bible readers.

The story begins in January, 1956. Jason Epstein, the young and energetic founding editor of Anchor Books (he was twenty-seven at the time), at the suggestion of Nathan Glazer, then a consultant to Doubleday, approached Albright about overseeing a series of brief introductions to books of the Bible. It was to be an interdenominational Bible, Glazer later recalled, a commentative work by scholars who had managed through their scholarship to escape religious and theological conflict.[138] Each volume in the series would be prefaced by introductory archaeological, theological, and philological background on the biblical book in question.[139] In March of that year, Freedman reported to Frank Cross that Albright had agreed to take part only if he (Freedman) would do the main editorial work. "It seemed to both of us," Freedman wrote, "that this was a rare opportunity to produce a unified work representing the Albright school or at least the Colloquium."[140] Freedman expressed the same view to Albright, and added that the new series would be an "eminently satisfactory substitute" for the Colloquium's moribund plans to publish a series of biblical commentaries. He thought it best to begin the new project with authors drawn from the Colloquium.[141]

This desire posed a problem, however, since there were not enough insiders to complete such a massive project, especially one that was to include the New Testament writings. Membership stood at thirteen in 1956, and although the additions to the founding eight were thought to be sympathetic with Albright's approach, they had much looser ties to him.[142]

Freedman suggested to Albright that they sign up members of the Colloquium right away. Next to be approached might be other former students of Albright, and finally, at the outer edge, "men sympathetic to our point

138. Nathan Glazer to Burke O. Long, August 13, 1992.
139. Jason Epstein to Albright, January 31, 1956.
140. Freedman to Cross, March 30, 1956, CDNF.
141. Freedman to Albright, March 31, 1956. See also Freedman to John Bright, March 17, 1956, CDNF.
142. The five new members were Bernhard Anderson, Walter Harrelson, James Muilenburg, B. Davie Napier, and R. B. Y. Scott.

of view and willing to work in harness," code language, I assume, for taking direction from the editors.

There was another difficulty too. From the beginning it was agreed that the new series should include Jewish as well as Christian authors. A letter of understanding with Doubleday stipulated the editors' intention to "include authors of the Catholic and Jewish faith as well as of the several Protestant denominations, since the series, while it will attempt to do justice to the religious content of the Bible, will not hew to any sectarian line."[143] However, all the members of the Colloquium at that time were Protestant, and while they differed somewhat in emphases and on particular theological points, they shared a broad interest in Protestant biblical theology and the conviction that historical study of the Bible was incomplete unless it helped shape religious appropriation of biblical teaching. Common experiences with Albright at the Johns Hopkins University enforced this broadly similar orientation.[144]

Moreover, despite the desire to include Jewish and Catholic participants in the project, early planning gave concrete form not to ecumenism, but distinctly Albrightean and Protestant concerns. For example, Freedman proposed that the book of Genesis be treated separately from other narratives such as those found in the book of Exodus. Genesis had long been a place for traditionalists and modernists to play out their ideological allegiances as objectivist debates over the "truth" or "falsity" of historical (dominantly Wellhausenian) criticism. For Albright, Genesis was also a battleground. He and his forces faced down opponents in the scholarly world, for example, on the question of how archaeology tended to confirm the historicity of the patriarchal traditions, or how certain ancient texts discovered by archaeologists supported the notion of an original poetic epic standing behind the prose narratives of Genesis.[145] Besides, this book perhaps more than any other had long been a site of explorations deep into the world of the ancient Near East. If the Albrightean "background approach" were to win out, it would have to win here. Although Freedman gave no reasons for his suggestion, it may have seemed natural that Genesis should be treated separately in the new series. Personal histories, reputations, commitments, and committed actions were at stake.

143. Freedman to Nathan Glazer, April 15, 1956. The letter did not mention any assignments for Jewish scholars, and noted only one, tentatively, "if possible," for a Roman Catholic scholar.

144. See David Noel Freedman, "W. F. Albright as Historian," in G. van Beek, ed., *The Scholarship of William Foxwell Albright: An Appraisal* (Atlanta: Scholars Press, 1989), 35.

145. See Albright, *The Archaeology of Palestine and the Bible; From the Stone Age to Christianity*, esp. chap. 1.

However, the second through fifth books of the Bible, Exodus through Deuteronomy, Freedman wrote to Albright, ought to be divided into two parts: one volume for the narratives on the exodus and wanderings of the Israelite ancestors, and a second volume for the legal and ritual materials once the narrative prose had been separated out. Moreover, the book of Daniel might be combined with Revelation, he suggested, since they belonged to the same literary genre.[146]

It is understandable that combining Daniel with Revelation would make sense as a practical matter. However, such expediency—it seemed innocently beyond question at the time—also implied ingrained ideological practice. The operative notion of "Bible" meant the Christian Bible, a hermeneutical construct that authorized reading disparate biblical writings in the hearing of each other, as parts of "old" and "new" testaments unified by a Christian consciousness. Moreover, Freedman's proposal to separate the narrative of redemption (exodus and wanderings) from the narrative of law (the reception of Torah and commandments) may have implied conventionally Protestant, and ultimately New Testament Pauline, values. This line of theological reasoning located the efficacy of God's redemptive activity primarily in historical process ("revelation in history"), rather than in the stabilities of eternal Torah, subject to human elaboration as instruction and law. Such an emphasis had gained prominence especially for Ernest Wright, at just the time Freedman and Albright were planning the *Anchor Bible*, partly under the influence of Gerhard von Rad, whose work in the history of narrative traditions offered major intellectual foundation for the postwar "biblical theology movement" in America.[147] Yet it was precisely this Protestant view, so natural to most Christian biblical scholars at the time, that effaced a potential conflict with commitments to an interfaith, collaborative effort. How were the theological sensibilities of Jews—it was not a question of overt sectarianism—to be included in the conceptual foundations of the project?

This latent conflict surfaced when Ernest Wright was consulted. More than any of Albright's sons at that time, Wright joined archaeological and

146. Freedman to Albright, March 31, 1956.
147. Gerhard von Rad, "Das formgeschictliche Problem des Hexateuch" (Beiträge zur Wissenschaft vom Alten und Neuen Testament, 4th series, vol. 26 [Stuttgart: Kohlhammer, 1938]); "Der Anfang der Geschichtsschreibung im alten Israel," *Archiv für Kulturgeschichte* 32 (1944): 1–42; "Die deuteronomistische Geschichtstheologie in den Königsbüchern," in *Deuteronomium Studien Teil B* (Forschungen zur Religion und Literatur des Alten und Neuen Testaments, New Series 40 [Göttingen: Vandenhoeck & Ruprecht, 1947]), 52–64. These and other works reached a culmination in *Theologie des Alten Testaments*, vols. 1 and 2 (Munich: Kaiser, 1957 and 1960). On the importance of "revelation in history" as a conceptual rubric, see Brevard Childs, *Biblical Theology in Crisis* (Philadelphia: Westminster Press, 1970), 39–44.

historical investigations (Albright's "background approach") to the needs and purposes of Christian theology. Thus the question of who was to be entrusted to shape the projected series, or exactly how "interfaith" would be reflected in volume assignments, was a crucial matter.

"I've hit the ceiling on a couple of things I've heard," he wrote to Albright in late June of 1956. Wright was opposed to the participation of two Jewish writers, Ephraim A. Speiser and H. Louis Ginsberg. Speiser had studied with James Montgomery, whom Albright much admired, at the University of Pennsylvania. In 1924 he wrote his Ph.D. thesis at Dropsie College under Max Margolis, also greatly appreciated by Albright.[148] Nearly the same age as Speiser, H. L. Ginsberg had taken his Ph.D. in Semitics from the University of London and in 1936 assumed his post at the Jewish Theological Seminary in New York. About five years earlier Speiser had been appointed professor concurrently at Pennsylvania and Dropsie. Ginsberg produced many philological studies of Aramaic and Ugaritic texts in relation to the Bible; he prized Albright's work, as Albright did his, and they enjoyed many occasions of professional association.[149] Speiser had distinguished himself in many technical fields of western Asia as well, and when discussions were under way about the *Anchor Bible*, he had already begun to devote much of his scholarly activities to literary and linguistic problems of the Bible.[150]

Suggesting that the inclusion of Speiser and Ginsberg might be "politically necessary," Wright nevertheless condemned it on the ground that the same sort of compromise had made a "hodge-podge" of the *Interpreter's Bible*.[151] Voicing high respect for Ginsberg, Wright nonetheless doubted that he could handle the "conceptual ideas or large perspectives such as are demanded in either history or theology."[152] He thought two Protestant members of the Colloquium, Bernhard Anderson and Walter Harrelson, would be much more suitable. In Anderson's case, it is not difficult to guess the reason, for he was about to publish a small book for lay people, *The Unfolding Drama of the Bible*[153] and a textbook, *Understanding the Old Testament*.[154] Both would codify for a broad audience of readers Albright's

148. See Albright's tributes to Margolis and Montgomery in *BASOR* 47 (1932): 35–36 and *Journal of Biblical Literature* 69 (1950): xviii–xix, respectively.

149. Albright's correspondence from the 1940s and 1950s amply testifies to their friendly and respectful relationship.

150. See S. David Sperling, et al., *Students of the Covenant: A History of Jewish Biblical Scholarship in North America* (Atlanta: Scholars Press, 1992), 71–73, 75–77.

151. Nashville: Abingdon-Cokesbury Press, 1951–57.

152. Wright to Albright, June 29, 1956.

153. New York: Association Press, 1957.

154. Englewood Cliffs, N.J.: Prentice-Hall, 1957.

emphasis on archaeologically informed background to the Bible and von Rad's theological appropriation of biblical narratives as *Heilsgeschichte*, or "salvation-history."

Freedman treated Wright's objections with great delicacy. When Albright had selected him to be coeditor of the series, Freedman had privately expressed his anxiety that Wright would feel slighted, especially since, as Freedman put it, the series "resembles very much an idea which he [Wright] has been pushing in the Colloquium for several years."[155] Freedman also seemed to know that Wright's objections, no matter how circumspectly he put them, were in some way theological. Given Wright's allegiance to Protestant theology, and his active participation in theological work—since the mid 1940s he had been very keen on publishing a theological dictionary of the Bible—he may have seen the Doubleday proposal, among other things, as an opportunity to cast biblical theology as recital of divine acts, or the "history of salvation."[156] While not overtly anti-Jewish, the enterprise did not attract Jewish biblical scholars, and its themes were heavily colored by Protestant paradigms of religion and faith, and attitudes of theological superiority toward Judaism after the rise of Christianity.[157]

Freedman seemed caught between Doubleday's ecumenical design for the project on the one hand, and Ernest Wright's theological interests on the other. The invitation from Doubleday offered a magnificent opportunity, but carried conditions that were not easy to reconcile with the interests and preferences of the Albright group.

Apparently unaware of the exclusionary elements implicit in his own design for the series, Freedman expressed the quandary and his unhappiness to Frank Cross, perhaps hoping that Cross could help mollify Wright. The assignment for Genesis would likely go to Ephraim Speiser, he wrote,

> who after the old man [Albright] and Mendy [Mendenhall] would
> be the best choice, and the exigencies of the situation dictate that

155. Freedman to Cross, March 30, 1956, CDNF.

156. Wright's *magnum opus* on this theme was about to be published: *The Book of the Acts of God: Contemporary Scholarship Interprets the Bible* (New York: Doubleday, 1957), co-authored with Floyd Filson.

157. See, for example, Wright's treatment of Abraham, not so much as religious hero as a "fallen" recipient of divine promise. Wright also downgraded law as a meeting point with God—this would be a theological perspective developed in rabbinic Judaism—in favor of God's saving *action* independent of, or at least prior to, the giving of law. (*Book of the Acts of God*, 61–98.) For a broader look at biblical theology as an implicitly and sometimes explicitly anti-Jewish endeavor, see Jon Levenson, "Why Jews Are Not Interested in Biblical Theology," in Jacob Neusner et al., *Judaic Perspectives on Ancient Israel* (Philadelphia: Fortress Press, 1987), 281–307.

we must have at least one prominent Jewish scholar, and of them all Speiser is the only one we could contemplate working with, and he has requested Genesis, for which you will admit he is admirably trained in all the necessary historical, archaeological, and linguistic disciplines, second perhaps only to Albright himself.

Freedman went on to report a telephone conversation with Wright, and as though putting his points to Wright through Cross, he wrote:

I hope you can recognize that in an operation of this kind, which is not precisely controlled by heilsgeschichtlich [salvation-history] enthusiasts (I mean the Anchor people), and which must of necessity be an interfaith undertaking, that some such arrangement as this was inevitable, if not the exact assignments as made, then something similar. You can't as Ernest suggested simply assign a couple of minor megillot [scrolls] to the Jewish scholars.[158]

Freedman sought a face-to-face meeting with Wright in early June.[159] Still unable to resolve the matter, Freedman later told Wright in a long letter that he wished to get "clearer in my own mind both your objections as to the approach of the men chosen for the books . . . and the specific points and attitudes you want to see preserved and expressed in the introductory material in such books."[160] The archaeological and historical data would be protected by Albright, Freedman continued, but Wright's reservations about whether the editors would be able to "secure an adequate expression of the conceptual point of view required for a proper appreciation of the religious orientation of the historical (and prophetic) books of the OT" was a more difficult matter. Freedman hoped that he could be given a fuller understanding of Wright's opinions, since the "hasty conversations we have had haven't been sufficient to give me a solid enough grounding to fight

158. Freedman to Cross, May 19, 1956, CDNF. Ephraim Speiser had been sounded out in May, 1956, to write the book on Genesis (Freedman to Albright, May 9, 1956), and Albright strongly concurred, commenting that Speiser was "the most conservative of competent Jewish Biblical scholars. . . . Besides, this would save us from any onus which may descend on us from conservative—or liberal—sides" (Albright to Freedman, May 11, 1956). In short, taking a politically sensitive decision now could spare the appearance of politics later! H. L. Ginsberg had been suggested by Glazer (Freedman to Albright, March 31, 1956).

159. Freedman to Wright, June 4, 1956.

160. Freedman to Wright, June 30, 1956.

such an item through." Finally he came directly to the point: the decision to include Jewish and Catholic writers was final.

> Of course you will say that it would be easier all around to have secured other men to write the books in question. I do not think this would have been possible, accepting the general terms of the Series, and the orientation involved, as well as Dr. Albright, and the inter-faith character of the Series.

Albright also held firm, but offered an immediate and conciliatory response to Wright's objections. Saying that his own first reaction about the project had been "very much like yours," nevertheless he thought that H. L. Ginsberg, who was being considered as author for the volume on Isaiah 1–39, "has been moving steadily to the right under the influence of Kaufmann. . . . Besides, H.L. would be much less satisfactory [than Muilenburg] for Isa. II."

One of the bases for this judgment might have been Muilenburg's literary sensitivities. Another, perhaps, was that the servant songs of Isaiah in chapters 40–55 were important to Christian theology, since they had been read by the early church and modern Christians, at various levels of intellectual sophistication, as prefigurations of the suffering Messiah, Jesus. These poems were thus crucial and traditional elements in the notion of Christian Bible, that theological unity of Old and New Testaments which had now been inscribed in the conceptual basis for the *Anchor Bible.* As for Speiser, he was Albright's choice for a different ideological reason. Albright asserted that he did not "know a single scholar outside our own immediate group" who was as able to handle background and translation issues with regard to the book of Genesis. In some ways, he added, Speiser would be "better than any of us."[161]

Nevertheless, Albright had expected certain difficulties in representing his own convictions to the reading public through these Jewish scholars, who after all were not among his direct scholarly offspring. Acknowledging that Speiser, for example, would very capably use Mesopotamian parallels to elucidate the Bible, Albright thought it obvious that Speiser would not be "*au courant*" with results of Palestine archaeology or, for that matter, with the latest on Egyptian parallels to the Bible. He might even dissent from Albright's views on the antiquity of the traditions in Genesis, since he was "still trying to hang on to a [Wellhausenian] literary approach as

161. Albright to Wright, July 2, 1956.

against [Albright's theory of] oral tradition and original poetic form."[162] A few weeks later, as discussions with Freedman continued, Albright offered an opinion on H. L. Ginsberg: "He will probably refuse to accept the second invasion in Hezekiah's time, in spite of the overwhelming evidence from Egyptian sources, and all of my other arguments."[163]

Despite these reservations, Albright expressed satisfaction in the Jewish authors who agreed to participate in the project: Speiser; his student Moshe Greenberg, who had received his Ph.D. just two years earlier; and Ginsberg. These men could be counted on to express conservative attitudes toward the text, Albright wrote to Freedman, and because they were deeply committed to studying biblical backgrounds, they were "probably the three best men in the country for our purposes from the Jewish side." He could understand Wright's being upset, Albright continued. But while denying Wright's suggestion that he and Freedman had been motivated primarily by political considerations, he nevertheless appeared to emphasize just the opposite. It was extremely important, he told Freedman, "not to seem in any way anti-Jewish," and to "try hard not to take a theological *parti pris*. . . . We could not possibly make the noncontroversial approach of the series clearer than by starting with Speiser [on Genesis]. Furthermore, he is *the* Jewish scholar who sympathizes most with our backgrounds approach."[164]

Despite the urgent tone and ideological stakes evident in early planning for the *Anchor Bible*, Freedman's hopes for the role that the early Colloquium might play were never quite realized. As volumes began to appear in the early 1960s, the involvement of the original members of the Biblical Colloquium turned out to be fairly negligible. Further, it will be recalled, new rules adopted in 1961 meant that membership began to broaden considerably beyond students of Albright. The ideological unity that Freedman, Albright, and others had sought in the *Anchor Bible* largely came down to one general point: Albright's definition of biblical study as incorporating in a primary way not literary studies of the text, but the results of archaeological and philological researches, his so-called "background approach."

The first published volume, Speiser's *Genesis*, was a nearly ideal Albrightean flagship for the series.[165] Albright could hardly have found much

162. Albright to Freedman, May 21, 1956. The theory of orally transmitted epic behind documents of the Pentateuch was articulated in its fullest form by Albright in his *Yahweh and the Gods of Canaan* (Garden City, N.Y.: Doubleday, 1968), 1–52.
163. Albright to Freedman, July 2, 1956.
164. Albright to Freedman, June 11, 1956.
165. E. A. Speiser, *Genesis*, Anchor Bible (Garden City, N.Y.: Doubleday, 1964).

that was offensive to his cherished convictions. While utilizing the results of archaeological excavations to illustrate the Bible, Speiser protected the Bible's privileged position in Jewish and Christian cultural perceptions. He put the Bible securely in its ancient Near Eastern environment, but, as a matter of generalized religious and cultural allegiance, he also reinforced its conceptual and spiritual superiority to its places of origin. Speiser basically accepted the historical reliability of the patriarchal traditions, while, like Albright, claiming the freedom to discard some textual details. He found a residue of the real Abraham in Genesis 14, an old touchstone for Albright. He praised the achievements of Moses as outlined in the book of Exodus and defended the antiquity of Israelite monotheism. Speiser read Moses as the privileged paradigm, and then pushed the limits of "antiquity" back to Abraham, whom he depicted as a kind of proto-Moses. Whether or not Albright liked this particular bit of speculation, he probably was not unhappy with the more basic implication. Even the narratives about the Israelite ancestors, so much a battleground in Bright's work against Alt and Noth, are important sources of reliable history and religious truth, that is, ethical monotheism.

To the extent that Speiser's volume was representative of what Freedman, Albright, and others from the Biblical Colloquium hoped to achieve, the *Anchor Bible* series at least started out as a testimony to the power of an Albrightean era. Seen as part of the story of the Biblical Colloquium, the series encoded many of the ideological debates and allegiances that authorized the Albrightean way and permeated the Colloquium's activities during that first decade. It was as though in their planting and reaping of Albright, members sought to create a fulfilled prophecy of G. Ernest Wright's words to Albright, that "the future belongs to your school of thought." Less self-consciously, the sons and grandsons of Albright gave social body to the way in which Albright constructed not only his object of research—ancient Near Eastern studies in the service of elucidating the Bible—but many of the underlying philosophical and theological convictions that energized and shaped a distinctive Albrightean culture of biblical studies.

Retrospective

Reconstructing these early activities of the Biblical Colloquium has offered me an opportunity to catch something of a social process through which knowledge about the Bible was created, codified, and disseminated. A

Harvard student recalled that Ernest Wright once dismissed a graduate seminar paper by declaring that the Biblical Colloquium would never accept the author's thesis. Reflecting on that incident with the sensitivities of the 1990s, the former student continued: "Ernest Wright thought the Biblical Colloquium was a political party. He didn't think it was a group of academics meeting to hash things out and go away different. It was one mind for him."[166]

While allowing for individual differences among the players, these sons of Albright transmitted and defended a recognizable Albrightean way. Their activities through the Biblical Colloquium's first decade illustrate what might be called a necessary condition for constructing knowledge: the use of power to maintain and defend social formations—in this case a "school" and its published research.

I have also spoken of interwoven ideological commitments involved in the building and maintenance of an Albrightean "school." A group of similarly trained scholars carried out their academic work significantly within the force field of their teacher. They followed Albright's commitments to modernist notions of positivistic science and its derived paradigms of biblical and archaeological study. For the most part they seemed to take up elements of Albright's narrative of intellectual revolution. Many sought to harness the power of that reformist impulse to serve Protestant theological purposes as well.

Vested production of knowledge, however, carries within itself a certain instability. Mainly by reading against the grain of Albright's myth of hermeneutical supplantation, I tried to situate Albrightean practice in relation to oppositional formations of social power, such as those Albright perceived at the University of Chicago. The Albrightean way carried within it internal tensions as well, resistive discourse of various kinds, which became visible above all in planning for the *Anchor Bible*. Ernest Wright's difficulties in coming to terms with the role of Jewish scholars is one of the more interesting of these internal ambiguities. From one perspective, the debates exposed a crack in the culture of Albrightean-styled biblical study. Ideologies of historical and philological science had suppressed religious difference, or supposedly made theological commitments irrelevant among scholars fervently devoted to scientific objectivity. Until, that is, a major publication of the Albright school was at stake.

More pronounced slippage along this same fault line had actually occurred some years earlier in connection with planning a dictionary of biblical languages. At that time, when World War II was coming to its close, the

166. Interviews, NELC.

challenge to the implicit canons of Albright's world were more direct, and in personal terms more anguishing, than debates over the *Anchor Bible*. Ernest Wright, never too far from energetic promotion of Christian theology and Albright's approach to the Bible, was again at the center of the conflict. So was Harry Orlinsky—friend of Wright, devoted student and colleague of Albright, and a Jew.

3   NOT WORDS ALONE
A Theo(philo)logical Dictionary

On July 21, 1944, a page 1 banner headline in the *New York Times* proclaimed Franklin Roosevelt's nomination as President for an unprecedented fourth term. News stories described "Allied gains everywhere," and an "almost successful attempt on Hitler's life." Americans at home began to envision how they might reclaim various enterprises deferred by the conflict.

That summer, Ernest Wright began dreaming of a new theological dictionary of the Bible that would help harvest all that Albright and his archaeological "background approach" had yielded. Wright was just seven years beyond his Johns Hopkins days, and had returned to his theological home in Chicago, the McCormick Theological Seminary. "It was ten, twelve years before I was weaned," Wright told Albright's biographer many years later. "I remained a student of Albright's—submitted everything I wrote to him before I printed it, that is, every serious thing, for about ten years or more."[1] Teacher and student shared academic gossip freely, and Albright offered generous instruction to, as Yigael Yadin wrote, Albright's "most beloved pupil," who was maintaining the Albrightean outpost among the Chicagoans.

Wright discussed his plans for a dictionary with Floyd Filson, an older colleague, professor of New Testament and dean of the seminary. A modest venture had been talked about and postponed in 1942. But this summer,

1. Running and Freedman, *Albright*, 218.

warmed by hopes of Allied victory and encouraged by L. J. Trinterud, the religious book editor of Westminster Press, Wright and Filson began to consult other scholars about a greatly expanded publication. By June of 1945, a formally organized editorial committee mapped out detailed plans for the project.

Wright wanted Albright to take responsibility for the Old Testament and Semitic languages components of the dictionary. Although very interested and supportive, Albright declined, citing his heavy commitments to other projects. He agreed, however, to serve on a supervisory committee. It was not enough to ease Wright's anxious second thoughts. "[The project] scares me because I am not the man to do it," he wrote to Albright. "I don't have the necessary linguistic training. So my job will have to be mostly editorial, while using the brains of the world's best men if possible."[2]

It was obvious to both that the dictionary needed help. They turned to Harry Orlinsky, a specialist in the language and history of the Hebrew and Greek versions of the Bible. Orlinsky had received his graduate training at the University of Pennsylvania and Dropsie College (Ph.D., 1935), and was then a teacher of Bible at the Baltimore Hebrew College. In the 1930s, Orlinsky and Wright met each other at the feet of Albright, a time that Wright would much later characterize as "the most wonderful days of my life."[3] Wright was finishing his Ph.D. thesis, and Orlinsky, a postdoctoral student under Albright, was a fellow by courtesy at the Johns Hopkins Oriental Seminary.

Like many others, Orlinsky was apparently captivated. In 1941, as a testimonial to Albright's fiftieth birthday, he worked virtually singlehandedly to produce an "indexed bibliography" of Albright's writings.[4] More than a list of publications, this labor of devotion represented Albright's work both as a scientific resource and as a compendium of the master's teachings. Indexes, with cross-references, excerpts, and subject headings, were so arranged that

    2. Wright to Albright, July 21, 1944. Some seven years later Wright still felt, perhaps even more acutely, inadequate in linguistic matters. Referring in mutual admiration to each other's theological work, Wright confided to John Bright, "It is the truth, though, that I really feel that I'm the dumb [s]quirt, and that most everybody is ahead of me. . . . But I guess it is Cross, Freedman, Mendenhall and Co. which get me. They are out of my class, and the chief reason is their linguistics and knowledge of and ability to read the inscriptions, etc. But I keep writing, getting the stuff printed—then wonder what the good men *really* think of the stuff!" Wright to John Bright, November 30, 1951. Courtesy Charles Bright.
    3. Running and Freedman, *Albright.* 202–3.
    4. H. Orlinsky, *An Indexed Bibliography of the Writings of William Foxwell Albright* (New Haven: The American Schools of Oriental Research, 1941). A committee of former students gave some help and advice, but entrusted the task to Orlinsky.

Fig. 8. Harry Orlinsky, ca. 1950.
Courtesy of the Hebrew Union
College-Jewish Institute of Religion,
New York.

a reader could "determine readily enough whether or not the author [Albright] has had anything new or corroborative to say about any given subject, and if so, exactly what, where, and when."[5]

Albright reciprocated the affection, and two years later praised Orlinsky as "learned, critical, judicious and meticulously accurate." He also judged him to be mature for his age, a "very successful teacher," an "extremely pleasant companion," and above all, he "has no bad habits and is a thoroughly human person."[6] To Stephen Wise, president of the Jewish Institute of

5. From the "Compiler's Introduction," v. With such aspirations for achieving authoritative status, this compendium could not be published without Albright's looking at the typescript. Wright, Nelson Glueck, and Abraham Sachs were troubled by Orlinsky's insistence on including brief epitomizing excerpts from Albright's writings in the index, but as in most matters at this stage in their respective careers, they acquiesced to Albright, who was "touched and pleased" by the undertaking. Even though protesting that the "selection from my writings, good and bad, is an undertaking worthy of a better cause," he offered no objection to its publication "substantially as it is." Albright to Wright, May 21, 1941.

6. Albright to Abraham Neuman, May 4, 1943. Albright had previously recommended Orlinsky to Neuman in similarly positive terms (Albright to Neuman, April 29, 1941).

Religion in New York City, Albright amplified the accolades: he had "great respect" for Orlinsky's judgment and found him so "uncompromisingly honest" that he relied upon him "constantly for advice and assistance." Bringing Orlinsky inside the Baltimore citadel, as it were, Albright added that even though Orlinsky took a modern historical approach to the Bible, he was "much more moderate in his views than the average so-called critical scholar."[7] Orlinsky had become, in effect, one of Albright's sons, a moderate ally against the radical critics.

When the opportunity came in 1944 to participate in preparing the new dictionary, Orlinsky readily agreed. It may have seemed as though conversations begun some two years earlier on plans for a modest Hebrew-English lexicon had simply resumed. By the spring of 1946, however, the project was floundering, and Orlinsky disengaged. When announcing his withdrawal, Orlinsky aimed his anger directly at the publisher:

> It is clear that my Jewishness prevents me from being named by Trinterud and his committee as editor of the Lexicon; if I were a Christian, there would have been not a moment of hesitation. As I wrote to you before, the Westminster people had the notion that they, compelled as they were, would hire Jewish scholarship for money, and suppress the Jewishness of the scholar on the title page. That will never be so.[8]

By reading events in terms of the suppressed Jewish expert, Orlinsky invoked a leitmotiv from the long history of ambiguous relations between Christian and Jewish students of the Hebrew Bible and other texts, such as the Talmud. Though immersed in the study of Jewish writings, many of these Christian Hebraists were deeply ambivalent toward Jews and Judaism, often looking on Jews as much-needed but unwelcome experts or as converts to Christianity whose "enlightenment" confirmed the truths of Christianity. In either case, many of these Christians defined Jews in complex ways, but principally as outsiders in a dominantly Christian realm.[9]

7. Albright to Stephen Wise, May 5, 1943.
8. Orlinsky to Albright, March 21, 1946.
9. For example, in the eighteenth century, Judah Monis was forced to convert to Christianity in order to teach Hebrew at Harvard (M. Klein, "A Jew at Harvard in the 18th Century," *Proceedings of the Massachusetts Historical Society* 97 [1985]: 135–45). Just over a century later, Isaac Nordheimer, whom Edward Robinson judged to be the finest Hebrew scholar of his generation, was not deemed fit to teach Hebrew at New York University. In 1838, when, owing

How had discussions about the Hebrew dictionary reached such an impasse that Orlinsky momentarily saw himself through an image from this discomforting history? How did the situation appear to Wright and Albright as they worked to develop the project, especially in the light of their warm feelings toward Orlinsky? Is it reasonable to believe, with Orlinsky, that the anti-Jewish burden of Christian Hebraism lingered on in at least this one program of publishing, or in the very practices of scholarly research it represented? What other dilemmas might this episode have posed for all parties, and especially for Albright, who was widely known for his support of Jews and other minorities?[10]

In seeking answers to such questions, some of the complexities of a small contest with much larger implications emerge. From one perspective, a Christian publisher wanting to sell books to a Christian public claimed the right to set a Christian's name prominently on the title page of the dictionary. From another angle, the action seemed oppressive, even anti-Jewish. Viewed from yet a third vantage point, the needs and desires of sectarian publishing encoded in the language of marketing fell together with the theologically interested discourse of biblical scholarship as practiced by the Albrighteans,

---

to Robinson's absence, Nordheimer was appointed instructor of sacred literature at Union Theological Seminary in New York, he was frequently challenged by other members of the faculty, all of whom had to profess the Westminster Confession, to defend his interpretations of the Bible. Remarkably, some of his colleagues seemed determined in their memoirs to portray him as a Christian, or *nearly* so, although he remained a Jew to the end of his short life (Shalom Goldman, "Isaac Nordheimer [1809–1842]: 'An Israelite Truly in Whom There Was No Guile,'" *American Jewish History* [December 1991]: 213–29). See also S. Goldman, "Professor George Bush: American Hebraist and Proto-Zionist," *American Jewish Archives* 43 [1991]: 59–69. For more general studies, see Jerome Friedman, *Michael Servetus: A Case Study in Total Heresy* (Geneva: 1978); idem, *The Most Ancient Testimony: Sixteenth Century Christian-Hebraica in the Age of Renaissance Nostalgia* (Athens: Ohio University Press, 1983); G. Lloyd Jones, *The Discovery of Hebrew in Tudor England* (Manchester: Manchester University Press, 1983); William McKane, *Selected Christian Hebraists* (Cambridge: Cambridge University Press, 1989); Frank Manuel, *The Broken Staff: Judaism Through Christian Eyes* (Cambridge, Mass.: Harvard University Press, 1992). See also an exhibition catalog, *Christian Hebraism: The Study of Jewish Culture by Christian Scholars in Medieval and Early Modern Times* (Cambridge, Mass.: Harvard University Library, 1988).

10. See Running and Freedman, *Albright*, 374–90. See Albright's essays "The Near East Needs the Jews," *New Palestine* 32:9 (1942): 12–13; "The Arabs and Jews," *Voice of Christian America* (National Conference on Palestine, American Palestine Committee, 1944), 18–22. Albright had not always been a Zionist. However, numerous letters during the years 1941–45 reflect his horror at Nazi treatment of Jews, and his becoming a strong supporter of an independent national home for the Jews. Such should not come at the cost of displacing Arabs already living in the area, however. Albright favored the United Nation's "two homeland" solution to the tension-filled legacies of European colonialism in the Middle East.

among others. Ernest Wright may have especially wanted a dictionary in part to establish a normative model of authentic scholarly knowledge: Albrightean competence in biblical background archaeology and philology joined to the interests of Christians and Christian theologians—in short, biblical theology as he understood it. Because they implied somewhat different foundational assumptions, Orlinsky's actions would have challenged that gesture of dominance, at least incipiently. However, the ideologies of scientific historical inquiry, which all parties shared and which presumed neutral space for scholarly practice, obscured such contested ground.

Although he called up the ghosts—or were they twentieth-century avatars?—of Christian Hebraists past, Orlinsky may have been somewhat exploited in ways other than those his angry outburst might suggest. Albright and Wright, while seemingly positioned within a circle of exclusionary privilege, may for their part be viewed as imprisoned by allegiances and alliances so natural to them as to remain practically invisible.

In the end, Orlinsky was left standing outside the door, and these particular issues remained unresolved. Although briefly challenged, the network of values and assumptions that seemed so second nature to Wright and Albright, even to Orlinsky in some measure, held firm. Yet, whatever its outcome, or lack of it, this incident may be read to yield Albrightean claims to normativeness and actions taken to assert its power in the social realm. What is visible in planning for the dictionary would come up again a decade later in the mid-1950s' Biblical Colloquium. As indicated above in Chapter 2, practitioners of a particular kind of linguistic craft—in this case, the social reality of Albrightean biblical scholarship—strove to maintain their place of privilege, and the objective, normative status of their particular claims to knowledge. Such is the way, as Foucault has maintained, that *all* knowledge is created and disseminated.[11]

A Hebrew Theological Dictionary

Envisioned as a postwar effort involving scholars on both sides of the Atlantic, the dictionary that Wright, Filson, Albright, and Trinterud were discussing in the summer of 1944 was to be an explicitly theological reference work based on the latest historical knowledge about biblical languages.

11. See, above all, Michel Foucault, *Power/Knowledge: Selected Interviews and Other Writings, 1972–1977*, ed. Colin Gordon; trans. Colin Gordon et al. (New York: Pantheon, 1980).

"Trinterud has given Filson and me the green light on a theological dictionary (2 volumes) of the Bible," Wright reported to Albright. He urgently wanted to join Filson in such a venture because, as he told Albright, "the job needs to be done, and there doesn't seem to be anybody else with the theological interest to do it."[12]

The dictionary had not always been thought of in such a self-consciously theological way. Two years earlier, Albright had discussed with Trinterud publishing a new Hebrew-English lexicon of the Old Testament that would take full advantage of information made possible by nearly a century of archaeological excavations. Harry Orlinsky may even have proposed such a venture—Albright referred indirectly to him—or perhaps Albright had conceived the dictionary with Orlinsky's participation in mind. In any case, Trinterud reported that he had been exploring the idea, "feeling our way slowly and talking it over with a number of our Old Testament professors."[13] He had sent a specimen page, a mock-up of a conventional philological lexicon, for Albright's inspection. However, owing to the "exigencies of war-time," he wrote to Albright, he was obliged to postpone further consideration. But he clearly wanted to keep the project alive. He hoped that the delay would not cause Orlinsky, to whom he apparently had not spoken, to lose "another opportunity while we are marking time," or that Albright himself would lose interest in the project.

Two years later, Trinterud was enthusiastic, and the project had taken on new dimensions—it was now larger, and explicitly described by Wright as "theological." In early December of 1944, Trinterud told Albright that he and others at the Westminster Press had informally agreed to "increase greatly the amount of subsidy which we would be willing to allot to the dictionary program." He believed he could secure additional commitments from two Presbyterian seminaries, Princeton and McCormick (where Wright taught), and a "Jewish group in New York," probably the Jewish Institute of Religion (Orlinsky's academic home).[14] Trinterud was eager to give flight to the venture, which had now grown to *three* volumes—one each on the Hebrew and Greek versions of the Old Testament, and a third for New Testament Greek.

The theological dimension of such a multivolume work must have seemed unremarkable at the time. In various retrospective looks at the field inspired

12. Wright to Albright, July 21, 1944.
13. Trinterud to Albright, May 29, 1942.
14. Trinterud to Albright, December 4, 1944.

by two major wars and prospects for world peace, Christian biblical scholars were noting a renewed interest in the Bible as theological resource. One wrote of the "death and rebirth" of theology, another of "reviving" interest in theology.[15] To Lutheran audiences, George Mendenhall extolled the "remarkable return to Old Testament theology."[16] Another writer saw the trend as evidence of a "growing conservatism," and warned that the excitement of recovery, while necessary to the "entire truth of the Bible," should not through undue enthusiasm abandon the gains made by the historical approach.[17]

When planning was renewed, the Hebrew dictionary seemed in part to reflect such widespread postwar excitement. The project drew its particular energies from Ernest Wright's discovery that he was, as Frank Cross remembered many years later, a "Reformed theologian,"[18] and from Trinterud's restless ambition to establish a commanding program of religious and scholarly publishing.

More than two years earlier, Trinterud had seen the new opportunities. He turned to the Albright circle, and on Albright's advice asked John Bright to write a book on biblical theology to fill a "crying need," as Bright put it.[19] At about the same time, during a summer of "four sermons and fifteen lectures on biblical theology" delivered to ministers, Wright stirred up something massive, passionate, and a little frightening within himself. "I let myself go more," he confided to Albright in the summer of 1942, "and get a bit fiery in making applications to the modern day." Anxious that he might degenerate into a mere popularizer, Wright sought reassurance from Albright. He admitted to the hold that the "neo-orthodoxy" of Karl Barth had on him.[20] As a German theologian coming to maturity soon after World War I, Barth stressed the absolute uniqueness of God's revelation and

15. James D. Smart, "The Death and Rebirth of Old Testament Theology," *Journal of Religion* 23 (1943): 1–11, 125–36; William A. Irwin, "The Reviving Theology of the Old Testament," *Journal of Religion* 25 (1945): 235–46.

16. "The Lutheran Church and Biblical Research," *Wittenberg Bulletin* (December 1947): 1–5.

17. Raymond A. Bowman, "Old Testament Research Between the Great Wars," in Harold Willoughby, ed., *The Study of the Bible Today and Tomorrow* (Chicago: University of Chicago Press, 1947), 3–31. Cf. the editor's comments, xiv. See in the same volume, Otto Baab, "Old Testament Theology: Its Possibility and Methodology," 401–18, and Amos Wilder, "New Testament Theology in Transition," 419–36.

18. "George Ernest Wright in Memoriam," *Newsletter of the American Schools of Oriental Research*, no. 3 (September 1974): 1.

19. Bright to Albright, April 22, 1942.

20. Wright to Albright, August 6, 1942. See G. E. Wright, "Neo-Orthodoxy and the Bible," *Journal of Bible and Religion* 14 (1946): 87–93.

redemption in Christ, the absolute righteousness and justice of God, and the inability of human beings to achieve good, or salvation, apart from God's power. His work expressed theologically the end of an earlier confidence in human progress, and so became a powerful restatement of orthodox dogma for a generation dispirited by two world wars.

It seemed so for Wright, who, continuing his letter to Albright, admitted that he was especially drawn to Barth's vibrant use of the Old Testament as Christian message. Despite disagreements with him, he accepted Barth's rendering of the "Biblical approach and point of view" as much preferred to the distant coldness of a rather bland American liberalism, that "modern washed out stuff." Albright encouraged his student in these new-found leanings,[21] and some two years later Wright published his first theological book, *The Challenge of Israel's Faith*.[22] He would go on to write many more, expressing what David Noel Freedman would eulogize as a "need to have theological reflection aspire to the dynamism of the prophetic presence in Israel."[23]

In November of 1944, Wright's new enthusiasm apparently spilled over into conversations with Trinterud, and their two ambitions met. He and Wright had spent an expansive and stimulating time together, Trinterud reported to Albright, "talking further about a Hebrew Dictionary and about the whole subject of biblical theology."[24] A few months later, they would discuss plans for a new journal devoted to biblical theology.[25] Excitement built, and in short order Wright and Filson would establish *Studies in Biblical Theology*, a series of postwar publications which announced itself—the words would be printed on the cover of each volume—as supplying theologically interested clergy and laymen with "the best work in biblical scholarship."[26]

21. Albright to Wright, August 10, 1942.
22. Chicago: University of Chicago Press, 1944. Letters confirm that Wright discussed the book extensively with Albright before it was published.
23. David Noel Freedman, "In Memoriam G. E. Wright," *Bulletin of the American Schools of Oriental Research* 220 (December 1975): 3. See Wright's declaration of Protestant principles in "The Christian Interpreter as Biblical Critic," *Interpretation* 1 (1947): 131–52. Among his later influential theological studies were *God Who Acts: Biblical Theology as Recital* (London: SCM Press, 1952) and, with Reginald Fuller, *The Book of the Acts of God* (Garden City, N.Y.: Doubleday, 1957); his last major theological work was *The Old Testament and Theology* (New York: Harper & Row, 1969).
24. Trinterud to Albright, November 10, 1944.
25. Wright to Millar Burrows, April 4, 1945; Wright to Albright, April 8, 1945.
26. The series, published by SCM Press, London, carried the quoted words on the inside cover of each volume.

Albright also was enthusiastic about Trinterud's "green light" for a theological dictionary. He had already been impressed by Trinterud's energetic approach to publishing—Albright was cooperating with Wright and Filson in another Trinterud project, a comprehensive historical (also theologically interested) atlas of the Bible.[27] About a year later he would speak of Trinterud as "revolutionizing American religious publication."[28] A theologically oriented lexicon could also provide Albright a welcome occasion to help advance what George Mendenhall, taking the lead from Albright himself, called "the tremendous task of starting anew the study of (Christian) Biblical Theology from the vantage point of newly won historical and religious knowledge of the entire Near-East."[29]

Albright's theological convictions, while not as explicitly proclaimed in print as Wright's, nevertheless were ever present elements in his research and teaching, and more importantly in two widely influential books that he published in the early 1940s. Writing as a Christian, Albright in *From the Stone Age to Christianity* constructed a narrative of how monotheistic religion emerged, under the purposive hand of divine guidance, from primitive gropings into full expression with Moses, passed through the biblical prophets who were the "summit of its spiritual evolution," and finally reached its unsurpassed achievement in early Christianity.[30] Albright's aim was nothing less than to trace "our Christian civilization of the West to its earliest sources," and, as the preface to the German translation stated, to "deliver a small contribution to Christian theology of the future."[31] In a

27. *The Westminster Historical Atlas of the Bible* (Philadelphia: Westminster Press, 1945). The preface made clear that the authors conceived the study of geography as a contemporary theological concern, aimed at understanding "the religious message" of the Bible, not merely the ancient religion of biblical peoples. In subsequent explanatory material, the authors gave much attention to biblical religion, but in such a way as to maintain its theological superiority over Canaanite neighbors, and to support its application as "message" to Christians in the modern church. Albright wrote an introductory chapter to the book, and played such a major role in its preparation that Wright and Filson made a private arrangement to share their royalties with him. Wright to Albright, July 19, 1943; Floyd Filson to Albright, November 22, 1946.

28. Albright to Walther Eichrodt, October 3, 1945.

29. George Mendenhall, "The Lutheran Church and Biblical Research," *Wittenberg Bulletin* (December 1947): 4.

30. Baltimore: Johns Hopkins University Press, 1940. See especially chap. 6, where Albright constructed a picture of Jesus and a Christianity that surpassed Greco-Roman and Jewish spirituality of the time.

31. *Stone Age*, 32. (Pagination refers to the Anchor Books edition [Garden City, N.Y.: Doubleday, 1967], in which the 1942 text was updated mainly with a new introduction and additional footnotes). The reference to "Christian theology" may be found in *Von der Steinzeit zum Christentum* (Bern: Francke, 1949), 7. The subdued but unmistakable evangelical substance may not have been irrelevant to Albright's plan to submit the manuscript to Abingdon Press

broader sense, the book was an elaborate apology for Christian claims, above those of Jews and Muslims, to high culture and appropriation of biblical revelation.[32] It was also a model, as one of Albright's students from the late 1950s aptly suggested, of what Albright considered proper religious study: not speculative philosophy or theology, but background archaeology and history of the Old Testament, and the study of its languages.[33]

Albright found Walther Eichrodt's theological writings a welcome ally in supporting such claims for the uniqueness and contemporary relevance of biblical (Christian) faith. They were also useful in fighting against the kinds of Christian reflection Albright found distasteful. Once Albright used Eichrodt's review of Harry Emerson Fosdick's *A Guide to Understanding the Bible* to counter what he considered Fosdick's "exceedingly disruptive tendency."[34] Fosdick ignored, claimed Albright, the revolutionary results of archaeological investigations, and relegated Moses to a primitive stage of religious development that was distant and disconnected to Christian (and Jewish) claims for exalted monotheism. Such attitudes were held by "the overwhelming majority of teachers of Bible in universities, seminaries and colleges," Albright told Eichrodt, and they must be combated, since they breed "little but contempt for the Old Testament."[35]

This charged reading of the religious-scholarly situation from the evangelical camp was certainly not lost on Trinterud. At about the same time, he thanked Albright not only for his assistance in the Wright-Filson *Atlas*, but also for "thrusting into the whole of American biblical literature a more scholarly and positive interpretation of the Christian Gospel."[36]

---

in competition for the Bross Award. The idea of a prize, Albright wrote to Ernest Wright, "interested Ruth [Norton Albright] so much that she read the entire book through twice, making innumerable suggestions for stylistic and logical improvement." She decided to "put up the cash for its publication," Albright continued, regardless of its fate in the Bross competition, and whatever the outcome of negotiations with Macmillan and Scribner's that were going on simultaneously. (Albright to Wright, June 17, 1940; see also, Albright to Wright, August 21, 1940.)

32. The seeds of *Stone Age* were already evident in an article Albright wrote for an evangelical Christian audience in 1922: "Archaeological Discovery in the Holy Land," *Bibliotheca Sacra* 79 (1922): 401–17.

33. Ray Cleveland to David Noel Freedman, June 13, 1973. From the files of Leona Running, referred to in the original typescript of Running and Freedman, *Albright*. I am indebted to Leona Running for this reference.

34. New York: Harper, 1938. Albright secured Eichrodt's critical review of Fosdick's book, wrote a long English summary, and published both in the *Journal of Biblical Literature* 65 (1946): 205–7. Albright to Walther Eichrodt, January 5, 1945. Later, with Trinterud's help he sought to publish an English translation of the review in *Theology Today*.

35. Albright to Eichrodt, October 3, 1945.

36. Trinterud to Albright, January 19, 1945.

Considering this coalescence of interests, it is perhaps not surprising that the project had become "theological" and that Albright pronounced Trinterud's plan just "splendid." It was "the sort of thing needed now, and just the kind of thing that can be done much better today than it could a few years ago," he wrote to Ernest Wright.[37] Eichrodt's *Theologie des Alten Testaments*[38] would make a "fine basis" for the dictionary, he continued, assuming necessary changes, "both to make it more suitable for Anglo-American readers and to bring it up to date archaeologically and philologically."

Implicit in this preference for Eichrodt's work was Albright's acceptance of the privileged place of Christians in defining what critical studies of the Bible should be. It was not that Jewish theological interpretations of the Bible were inappropriate, or that Albright was disrespectful of religious differences. Quite the opposite, as many have testified.[39] Albright believed that historical criticism, with its appeal to universal reason and objective truth, could extricate itself from the particulars of religious commitment without devaluing the absolutist claims of faith. "Lecturing as I do constantly to Catholic priests and theological students, Protestant ministers and seminaries, and to Jews of all types and descriptions," he once wrote to William Graham, "I can see the merit of a common intellectual approach, which honestly faces the absolute differences of religious viewpoint and recognizes merit in each without surrendering one's own religious convictions in any respect." He took, Albright continued, an "intellectual position, not a religious one," but he thought he could see definite religious values in it for religious people of all types.[40]

Yet, the assumption that an "intellectual" position could be quarantined from "religious" commitment was a conviction that, for Albright and Eichrodt and many others, expressed itself in a powerful sectarian gesture: claiming the center for the language of historical scholarship in support of Christian sensibilities. Convinced of the higher truth of the *Christian* reading of the Bible, they created interpretations of biblical peoples that subtly devalued hermeneutical pathways which nonmessianic Jews had developed since the early days of Christianity.

Eichrodt, for example, saw a "purposive movement" of revelation through the deadening postexilic period toward a "manifestation in Christ," a move-

37. Albright to Wright, July 24, 1944.
38. Leipzig: Hinrich's, 1933–39.
39. Running and Freedman, *Albright*, 374–90.
40. Albright to William Graham, March 11, 1938.

ment which to him—Eichrodt's historical and descriptive language suggests that *anybody* should see this point—is evidenced in the "*torso-like* appearance of Judaism in separation from Christianity" (emphasis added).[41]

Similarly, Albright mapped the course of monotheistic belief to its highest point in the religion of Jesus, which, in more conventional theological language, meant that the religion of the New Testament was the "extension and fulfillment" of the Old Testament.[42] What of the Jews, such as the ancient Pharisees, who saw their own extension in the creation and interpretation of other scriptural texts, such as Mishnah and Gemara (Talmud)? Although he "wholeheartedly" welcomed the "rehabilitation of the Pharisees" in scholarly work of the war years, Albright nevertheless silenced and subtly denigrated them in *Stone Age*. He accomplished this effect not by engaging Pharisaic sources directly, but by working into the weave of his historical narrative of monotheism certain fundamental theological (Protestant) constructions that followed an age-old logic of displacement: faith over works, interiority of spirit over externals of law.

These presumptive "truths," or valorized concepts, made it easy for Albright to adopt apparently without much question many of the polemical New Testament attitudes toward the Pharisees, and to perpetuate the long history of theological ambivalence toward religious claims made by Jews. Albright passed on, for example, a popular notion that Jesus acted out of the richness of inner spirit, while the Pharisees concentrated on less approved, and somehow less genuine, externalities of action. On this conceptual scaffolding, in a seeming blend rather than separation of "intellectual position" and "religious conviction," Albright wrote that Jesus' hostility toward the Pharisees "was based mainly on His profound sympathy for the poor and suffering, to whom the Pharisees as a group showed charity but scant sympathy, feeling in typically puritanical fashion that their misery must somehow be the result of sin."[43]

41. Walther Eichrodt, *Theology of the Old Testament*, vol. 1, trans. J. A. Baker (Philadelphia: Westminster Press, 1963), 26.
42. *Archaeology and the Religion of Israel* (Baltimore: Johns Hopkins University Press, 1942; 5th ed., 1968), 4.
43. *Stone Age*, 391–92. Although Albright condemned anti-Semitism, like many Christian scholars of the time he seemed to believe that a profession of superiority for Christian religion would somehow be taken as an unambiguously benign act toward Jews and Jewish theology. Once he was asked to comment on A. C. Knudsen's opinion that Jesus fulfilled the law and the prophets by raising them to a plane of "absolute ethical perfection," leaving behind notions of God that were bound to nationalism, legalism, and particularism. One might have thought that Knudsen implicitly rebuked rabbinic developments out of this same tradition, but Albright

This Christian theological ethos, which fairly encompassed most biblical scholars during the postwar years, provided the setting in which the new Hebrew theological dictionary took shape. That same ethos might be seen, then, as potentially problematic for any Jewish scholar, whether theologically interested or not. And so it proved to be, although at the time not so clearly recognized as a late-twentieth-century perspective, with its heightened sensitivity to ideological difference, allows.

A Theo(philo)logical Dictionary?

As discussions advanced, Wright brought Orlinsky into a more direct engagement with the project. They met with Trinterud in late 1944 and discussed their plans. The dictionary now included a fourth volume, devoted to essays on "biblical thought." After the meeting, Orlinsky seemed a little hesitant. The project was still vaguely defined and as yet it had not been formally adopted by the publisher. If he had other misgivings, they were overcome by Wright's infectious enthusiasm. "I'd like very much to do it, and so would Wright like to start on his volume," he wrote to Albright. "I'll betcha we'd all put out the best handbooks available."[44]

Discussions soon became more formal. Trinterud organized a "Committee on Theological Lexicons," consisting of himself and five Protestant biblical scholars: Wright, Filson, Albright, Millar Burrows, professor of Bible at Yale Divinity School, and Henry Gehman, professor of Semitic languages, Greek, and Old Testament at Princeton Theological Seminary. A first meeting was set for June 29, 1945, at which time it was expected that sufficient planning could be concluded for Trinterud to secure final authorization of the project from the senior staff at Westminster Press.

Meanwhile, as private conversations continued, Wright and Orlinsky became anxious. They had understood that Orlinsky would write the Hebrew dictionary, and that Wright would simply edit his work. But Trinterud's actions now seemed to imply some misgivings about Orlinsky's role in the project. As far as I can see, the altered conceptual ground of the project,

---

replied simply: "I have no objection to Knudsen's statement. I knew him years ago and was impressed with his fine attitude." (Albright to Edwin Ross, September 14, 1943.) For Knudsen's comments, see "The Old Testament Conception of God," in Frederick Eiselen et al., *The Abingdon Bible Commentary* (New York: Abingdon, 1929), 164.

44. Orlinsky to Albright, December 29, 1944.

from Hebrew dictionary to "Theological Lexicons," had created a new point of vantage from which Trinterud would view Orlinsky's participation.

In late winter of 1945, Orlinsky was dismayed that Trinterud had made an inept appeal for support from the Jewish Institute of Religion. Trinterud's letter to Dean Slonimsky asking for a $5,000 contribution failed to mention two matters of great importance, Orlinsky told Wright: that Slonimsky's school was to be "the only Jewish institution represented in a Christian scholarly project," and that one of its faculty members was to write the Hebrew dictionary. The latter point, Orlinsky wrote, was the "most important" omission in Trinterud's botched proposal, and particularly upsetting because he should have fully understood how crucial a factor Orlinsky's role in the project would be to the dean. Besides, he continued, "I stressed during our luncheon talk at the Hopkins Faculty Club . . . and with which Albright and yourself agree, namely, that I was to do the Hebrew Lexicon. This is essential, because why should the Institute fork over so much money for someone else to get all the scholarly glory?"[45] Telling Wright that he had intervened with Dean Slonimsky, Orlinsky hoped that he had corrected the misapprehension and cleared the way for a positive response. He may very well have been a little suspicious, however. Why would Trinterud *not* have forthrightly mentioned Orlinsky's role? Was he unaware of, or unsympathetic toward, Wright's and Orlinsky's division of labor? Was he equivocating on the matter? Or had he simply made a mistake in approaching Dean Slonimsky?

A few months later, according to Albright, Stephen Wise, president of the Jewish Institute of Religion, was informed that a subsidy was no longer necessary, since Trinterud had secured adequate funds for the project.[46] A few days earlier Orlinsky had reported a rumor to that effect, but had expressed his doubts that Trinterud had really raised all the money necessary for the project.[47] Apparently anxious to head off tensions or misunderstandings, Albright then urgently responded "because of the Hebrew Dictionary" (he had marked the "rumor" paragraph in Orlinsky's letter), and affirmed that Trinterud had raised the necessary funds. He then dealt with what he took to be a suspicion implied in Orlinsky's doubts: "This has nothing to do with your participation in the project, so far as I know."[48]

Meanwhile, Wright reported to Albright that Trinterud had put forward an editorial plan that was "difficult to turn down, though it isn't quite what

45. Orlinsky to Wright, February 22, 1945.
46. Albright to Orlinsky, May 13, 1945.
47. Orlinsky to Albright, May 10, 1945.
48. Albright to Orlinsky, May 13, 1945.

we had originally thought it to be." Wright gave no details; perhaps he got none from Trinterud at the time. In any case, he added only that "for a number of reasons" Trinterud was opposed to a single author for any of the dictionaries. He wanted a "coalition to work on each book."[49]

Two weeks later, Wright was forthright about the new plan and the dilemmas it posed for him. "Trinterud wants all three language lexicons heavily weighted on *theology*," he confided to Albright. "The result is that he most emphatically does not want to give full or sole charge of [the] Hebrew lexicon to Orlinsky or any Jew. He's willing for Orlinsky to have a large place in it, but he insists [he] be balanced by men who insist on and are actually interested in Christian theology." Trinterud's "coalition," at least in part, would obscure the ideological boundary he had drawn around the project even as it would have Orlinsky participate unawares under circumscribed conditions. Or, as explained by Wright,

> [Trinterud] has suggested that Filson and I become Gen'l Editors of [the] whole series and *to work with linguists* on the Hebrew & Greek N.T. lexicons, pulling in one or more Europeans to help out. While it flatters and interests me greatly, I am appalled at my linguistic inadequacy for the job. Maybe we could get one or two Europeans to do theological words, subject to Orlinsky's going over? Maybe I could parcel out theological words to a number of different scholars, and get [the] result back for checking with Orlinsky?[50]

Trinterud's insistence seemed to squeeze Wright into a narrow space. His plan removed Orlinsky from direct responsibility, thus violating the informal understandings that Wright and Orlinsky had come to, and yet it did nothing to diminish Wright's need for Orlinsky's expert knowledge of Semitic languages. In some way the dictionary would have to be an Orlinsky project, but could this merely entail Orlinsky's "checking" the work of others? And besides, what of the friendly and respectful relationship the two men had enjoyed since their days at Johns Hopkins?

Wright hoped that some solution to his quandaries could be found before the editorial committee met on June 29, when it would deal with Trinterud's proposal. Although by Wright's own account he argued strenuously against

49. Wright to Albright, May 22, 1945.
50. Wright to Albright, June 6, 1945. I have been unable to locate any of Trinterud's records among the archives of Westminster Press. Although still living, Trinterud is frail, suffering from dementia, and unable to respond to inquiries.

the "coalition" idea, it is nowhere evident that he rejected the plan, earlier described as "difficult to turn down," or that he suspected that it might be, at least in part, an ideologically charged move to limit Jewish presence at the center of the dictionary project.

It is possible that Trinterud's concerns came down to the basics of marketing. He may have simply wanted to produce a dictionary that would be purchased by his largest audience: Christian scholars and clergy and ministers-in-training, especially Presbyterians and Lutherans for whom study of the original biblical languages was still highly valued. For this purpose, perhaps, he thought that Wright's name, rather than Orlinsky's, would be critical. Yet, as Wright saw it, Trinterud wanted some kind of advocacy too, "men who *insist on* and are actually *interested in* Christian theology." It was this point that exposed a crack in the delicate structures of biblical criticism as practiced by the Albrighteans at the time.

In effect, Trinterud's demand clashed with a belief that Albright, Wright, and many other biblical scholars, even Orlinsky himself, firmly espoused. Historical and linguistic study of the Bible could be carried out with such rigor as to aspire to be free of anachronisms and sectarian religious bias. Indeed, a short while later the editorial committee of the lexicon affirmed its own adherence to this ruling ideology of scientific research, the master narrative of objective knowledge-making. Each definition in the dictionary should "bring out the religious or theological meaning of the word," and "traditional theological terms, e.g., faith, salvation, and so forth may be used in these definitions but [they] shall always be so employed and so interpreted as to guard against any reading back of later ideas into the Biblical terms."[51]

Such convictions lay at the heart of Albright's assumption that an "intellectual," not a "religious," position on scholarly matters could be taken by properly trained, scientifically minded scholars of the Bible. Something similar probably lay embedded in Wright's musings that, given Trinterud's insistence on a "coalition," perhaps one person could "do theological words" and the work submitted to disinterested scrutiny, that is, be "subject to Orlinsky's going over." However, if a Jew, *any* Jew, must be excluded from having "sole charge," and his influence be checkmated by "men who insist on . . . Christian theology," then the Hebrew Bible and its language was by implication to be read not as an *ancient* document, as presumed by the dogmas of scientific investigation, but as a *Christian* text, sanctioned by

---

51. Minutes of Committee on Theological Lexicons, June 29, 1945, with a cover letter from L. J. Trinterud to Albright, September 28, 1945.

Christian knowledge makers. Thus one set of ideological principles, the Bible read as source of Christian revelation and theology, would displace another, the Bible investigated and mastered scientifically, as ancient object.

As will be seen, Albright and Wright may not have noticed the conflict between these competing interests because they had adopted a mediating ideology: search for religious truth does not conflict with scientific knowledge; or put another way, disinterested search for objective truth about the Bible is not necessarily compromised by religious conviction. The "religious" could be kept separate from the "intellectual." As one of Wright's students from the early 1960s put the matter, by doing scientific archaeology, by sorting out the actual history of ancient Israel, "Wright lived the synthesis." He believed that he was actually grounding theology, which he took to be faith interpretations of real events, on objectively established facts of history. "I think Wright felt that when he did archaeology, he was contributing in a pretty direct fashion to biblical theology that was grounded in what really happened."[52]

Ernest Wright, like Albright, could hardly reject the principle implied in Trinterud's boundary around the project. Both were very much committed to reading the Bible for its theological relevance to modern Christians. And yet, each was personally committed to Orlinsky, and to the understandings they had reached among themselves. In agonizing over the dilemma, in trying to hold on to conflicting allegiances, neither Wright nor Albright seemed to notice the degree to which their faith in objectivist scholarship had been rendered problematic. If the project were to guard against anachronisms, why could not a Jew do the job as well as a Christian? Or was a Jew somehow alien to the center, and thereby to be contained or kept at the margin?

When it met on June 29 the editorial committee ratified Trinterud's scheme. There were to be four volumes: "A Theological Lexicon of Biblical Hebrew"; "A Theological Lexicon of the Greek of the Septuagint"; "A Theological Lexicon of the Greek of the New Testament"; and "A Lexicon of Biblical Thought." Each dictionary was to be put in the hands of three editors, headed by an American scholar, with the aim of achieving a "well-balanced

52. Interview with a graduate of the Harvard program in Near Eastern History and Civilizations, 1994. See a recent discussion of Wright's theological efforts in Leo G. Perdue, *The Collapse of History: Reconstructing Old Testament Theology* (Minneapolis: Fortress Press, 1994), 19–44. For an appreciation of Wright's contributions to archaeology, treated separately from his theological work, see Philip J. King, "The Influence of G. Ernest Wright on the Archaeology of Palestine," in Leo Perdue et al., eds., *Archaeology and Biblical Interpretation: Essays in Memory of D. Glenn Rose* (Atlanta: John Knox Press, 1987), 15–29.

trio of editors who would be able to supplement each other's linguistic, historical, and theological abilities." Furthermore, in what was to be a critical decision for Orlinsky, the names of these three editors were to appear on the title page, in an order that reflected their relative responsibilities. Wright was elected chief editor of the Hebrew dictionary by the all-Christian committee, which also recommended that Wright consider Harry Orlinsky as one of the two additional editors.[53]

Wright and Filson quickly met with Orlinsky and apparently were able to report on the situation in such a way as to keep Orlinsky involved and ignorant of Trinterud's insistence. Perhaps Wright still hoped to find a way to recognize what he knew was to be Orlinsky's major contribution without offending Trinterud's strictures against it. Orlinsky later told Albright, as though nothing more than recognition was at stake, that he had "no qualms about who will get credit for what." He might not be willing to work with other people who lacked his full confidence, but "with people like Burrows, Gehman, and yourself, and the others on the Committee, and with such a 'saint, gentleman, and scholar' as Ernest is, I am willing to go all the way to the best of my ability."[54] Albright privately expressed relief to Wright about this outcome.[55] Yet the basic points of tension with Trinterud, about which Orlinsky was apparently unaware, had not been eliminated. In historical hindsight, one may wonder if some of the unease in the situation derived from playing a variant on an ancient theme of Christian Hebraism: Christian participants define the Jew in their midst as alien though necessary, fraught with ambiguous potential that requires restriction and containment.

In any case, despite the optimistic spirit of that meeting with Orlinsky, Wright seemed to recognize the lingering cloud of unresolved issues. In October, he reported to Albright, he had proposed a "compromise" to Trinterud. The scheme [Ernest Wright as editor in chief] would be acceptable as a working arrangement, if somehow the title page reflected the actual situation, namely, that Orlinsky would be responsible for the linguistic and philological accuracy of the dictionary. But how could this recognition be achieved? Would Wright and Orlinsky be listed as "coeditors"? Or would Wright be noted as "general editor" and Orlinsky as "chief author"? Whatever may have been proposed exactly, Trinterud apparently did not yield, for Wright went on to exclaim, "*I'd give anything* to get out of the

53. Minutes, June 29, 1945.
54. Orlinsky to Albright, July 2, 1945.
55. Albright to Wright, July 18, 1945.

Hebrew lexicon altogether. Trinterud *insists* that I've got to be general editor of that volume, and that Orlinsky can be nothing more than an Associate Editor—and that even includes the title page of the book, if and when it appears."[56]

Wright tossed and turned, and found no rest in his anguished letter to Albright. He was frustrated at his failure to move Trinterud ("I've spent hours arguing with him about it"); and how could he face Orlinsky with such an arrangement? He probably would quit, and justifiably so, but then what would happen to the whole enterprise? he fretted. On the other hand, Trinterud's position did not seem exactly unreasonable—he wanted these volumes to be unique in the marketplace, and distinctly theological, after all, and so was "most emphatic that he will not publish an Orlinsky dictionary," because he wanted someone with "the theological bug to head it up and set the tone." To whom could he turn? "Rightly or wrongly," Wright told Albright, "I am the only one he wants to trust with it."

Having forgotten, or suppressed, his report that Trinterud refused *any* Jew to head the project, and now implying that such refusal was merely a matter of excluding one particular Jew who lacked a "theological bug," Wright finally returned to the conflicting demands that had crept into the situation. He put the dilemma squarely before Albright:

> If Orlinsky won't get in on the job, then the heart and core of the Hebrew dictionary falls out, and I see no use of our doing it. But how can Orlinsky come in by the arrangement Trinterud is insisting on without feeling unhappy about it. I feel it is unfair. Yet Trinterud insists that the main man must be one who is interested in Christian theology.

The repressed element returns, yet unspoken. Orlinsky lacked more than a "theological bug." He could, naturally enough, not offer *Christian* biblical theology in a Christian reference work. Recognizing him as anything more than "associate editor" would seem to weaken that Christian presumption. And yet, how could both Wright's and Orlinsky's contributions be honestly shown? Also—this was perhaps one unrecognized source of Wright's dilemma—Orlinsky could not offer interpretive biblical theology of the type to which Wright himself had become deeply committed, and had begun to build on the foundations of historical and archaeological researches.

---

56. Wright to Albright, October 17, 1945.

Wright was especially worried about how little the Old Testament was used in churches, which, in his view (it was Albright's view as well), had been deadened on the one hand by decades of fundamentalist literalism and on the other by arid, even antireligious, historical criticism of the Bible.[57] Wright possibly thought that the proposed theological dictionaries, part of the wave of theological renewal, could help change that situation. Indeed, in a theological book published just a year earlier, Wright laid the blame for such a dispirited scripture at the feet of biblical scholars on the one hand who work with "dissecting detachment," and on the other hand, systematic theologians who "go to the Bible for purely illustrative purposes." The correct approach was to blend religious commitment with objectively founded historical criticism, and so restore the Old Testament as direct address to contemporary believers.[58] Given the restricted intellectual environment in which Ernest Wright worked—the Presbyterian Church in America, with its roots in Calvinist tradition—this prescription meant in practice that Wright was to lift up the Word of God as it was addressed specifically to Christians.

Albright offered encouragement to Wright, since, as it will be recalled, he himself mapped the territory of a theologically committed biblical studies with similar landmarks. Advances in archaeology and scientific study of Semitic languages rescued the Bible from the desert-dry criticism of literary scholars who divided biblical narratives into fragments of lost source documents, or who separated out original textual material from later additions with little reference to linguistic evidence from outside the Bible. Such scholars are blind to innovative progress purchased by the objective and scientific information rapidly accumulating from archaeological excavations. In the new era, there arises a Bible freshly perceived as historically reliable and theologically relevant, especially when put into a master narrative, such as *Stone Age,* which authorized biblically centered Christian claims to higher culture, religion, and philosophy.[59]

The proposed dictionary, then, was consistent with an underlying theological concern in Albright's writings, and it coincided with Wright's passionate turn to Christian biblical theology. It was not a project that they, especially Wright, would easily let go. Rather, it would become, at least in prospect, a

57. For a broad account of the "biblical theology movement" that emerged in postwar America, with Wright cast as a central player, see Brevard Childs, *Biblical Theology in Crisis* (Philadelphia: Westminster Press, 1970), 14–50. See also Leo G. Perdue, *The Collapse of History.*
58. Wright to Albright, September 2, 1943. The book in question was G. Ernest Wright, *The Challenge of Israel's Faith* (Chicago: University of Chicago Press, 1944).
59. See above, Chapter 2, "Planting and Reaping."

prime exemplar of how Wright and others, chiefly Presbyterians, yoked the methods of historical criticism to their desire to build renewed reverence for the Bible and shape its appreciation as a theological resource. The confusion implied in joining the historian's (or archaeologist's) assumptions about objective, "factual" truth with a religious believer's commitment to extracting *ahistorical* religious truths from their encasement in biblical (historical) events, was glossed over. It was simply assumed, without argument, that a historically described and, for the Albrighteans especially, an archaeologically, philologically "backgrounded" Bible contributed a firm and nonspeculative base for constructive theology. Put another way, a properly understood Bible yielded what biblical writers actually meant to say (ancient Israel's theological truths), and these truths, since they were also eternal verities of God, naturally could be relied on for Christian theology.

Since his views were largely congruent, Albright encouraged Wright to hang on to both the dictionary project and Orlinsky's participation in it. He apparently took it for granted that Orlinsky could offer the "objective" linguistic basis on which to build. "Stick to your guns on the Orlinsky matter," he wrote. "I'll support you strongly whenever I get a chance. Get [Millar] Burrows to do the same." Evaluating other scholars who might be invited to join the project, Albright preferred some sort of Wright-Orlinsky team if Trinterud's "coalition" approach had to be accepted. None of the other possible participants could "compare with Orlinsky in competence and common sense, and none of them has your neo-orthodox point of view or your common sense (owing largely to a sound archaeological background)."[60]

Orlinsky, however, seemed less at ease, and would in time press his concerns. Committed to the modernist assumptions of historical "science," he believed that one could lay hold of objective facts about the past on the basis of a rigorous application of rational principles of discovery and evaluation of evidence. For a dictionary, one would describe the meaning of biblical words strictly in their ancient context. By all appearances sharing these historicist assumptions with Albright, Wright, and other members of the lexicon committee, Orlinsky was nevertheless wary of anachronistic theological dogmatism. Wright and Albright rejected dogmatism as well, but nonetheless clung to a conviction that reasoned historical description could avoid this failing and still serve the needs of contemporary theological construction. This was the outer gate of the Baltimore citadel. Inside, protected and not quite visible to planners of the dictionary, was another bulwark:

60. Albright to Wright, October 19, 1945.

the insistence of privileged normativeness for the Albrightean approach to biblical studies. Orlinsky, in his own way, would challenge both.

Somewhat obscure in planning for the dictionary, one of the points of conflict had actually surfaced with some clarity a few years earlier. Orlinsky wrote a review of Charles T. Fritsch's study of how Hellenistic translators of the Hebrew Bible avoided representing God with human characteristics and emotions such as "hand," "face," "eyes," or "anger."[61] Fritsch should have proved that such Hebrew expressions were really anthropomorphisms or anthropopathisms before he assembled, classified, and discussed them as such, Orlinsky said. He went on to demonstrate, at least to his satisfaction, that had Fritsch not assumed the Greek translators to be "anti-anthropomorphic," that is, theologically motivated to substitute more abstract expressions for the deity's human characteristics, then he could have followed a consistently rigorous and scientific method in assembling the evidence. In such a case, Fritsch would not have missed the proper linguistic, objective conclusion: "What is involved is not theology [the theological beliefs of Hellenistic Jewish translators] but stylism and intelligibility," in short, the concerns of any translator.[62]

When Orlinsky questioned the assumption on which Fritsch's study proceeded, he came close to exposing a conceptual structure that had become standard, though implicit, in many expositions of Christian theology. It was often claimed or assumed that Hellenistic Jews, who were under the influence of Greek habits of conceiving of God in abstract, bodiless terms, had begun to make God impersonal and distant, removed from the cares and needs of ordinary human beings. Such a generalization had just enough textual basis to take on the status of naturalized "fact," and thus came to support unproblematically a value-laden view of early Christianity: Jesus and the church, God's incarnation in a man, bridged that increased gulf between human and divine and reclaimed in both concept and divinity (Word)–made–flesh the saving intimacies of a loving, forgiving, redeeming "Father."[63]

61. *The Anti-Anthropomorphisms of the Greek Pentateuch* (Princeton: Princeton University Press, 1943). The review appeared in the *Crozer Quarterly* 21 (1944): 156–60. I am indebted to John Huddlestun for this reference.

62. Orlinsky, "Review of Fritsch," 159.

63. Recent discussion of the Aramaic word *'abba,* "father," and its use by Jesus to mean "daddy" or "father dear," thus marking a break with allegedly more formal Jewish usage, possibly involves similar apologetic Christian interests. See J. Jeremias, *Abba: Studien zur neutestamentlichen Theologie und Zeitgeschichte* (Göttingen: Vandenhoeck & Ruprecht, 1966), which was republished substantially in English as *The Prayers of Jesus* (Naperville, Ill.: Allenson, 1967). James Barr ("Abba isn't 'Daddy!' " *Journal of Theological Studies* 39 [1988]: 28–47) not

Orlinsky, of course, did not follow this line of argument in his review. Yet, if Fritsch were to have questioned or even given up his assumption that the Greek translators were indeed "anti-anthropomorphic," what then of the larger construct, the long-standing theological interest in depicting the Hellenistic Jewish world in need of correction? Orlinsky's work was not necessarily antitheological or antireligious. But it could be perceived as such by persons who might confuse his allegiance to a radically descriptive method (what were the translators actually doing in their translations?) with rejection of religious thought (the translators were concerned in this instance not with theology but with rendering idiomatic Hebrew intelligibly into Greek). Orlinsky invoked one ideological perspective, the canons of scientific philology, in such a way that Fritsch would be challenged to justify his own commitment to a different, or competing, ideology: a supersessionist Christian revelation.

I do not know whether Fritsch responded to Orlinsky's criticisms at the time. However, about a decade later he published a harsh review of Orlinsky's *Ancient Israel*.[64] Fritsch's essay carried within its rhetoric of criticism and dismissal those same, perhaps naive, commitments to polarized choices, valued differently: Is one to engage in *theologically* or *scientifically* interested scholarship? Moreover, private exchanges at the time suggest that some of the burdens of Christian and Jewish cooperation, so evident in planning for the theological lexicon, still fractured the discourse of Albrightean scholarship.

Fritsch noted in the opening sentence of his review that it had been a good idea to include a book on ancient Israel in a series covering the development of Western civilization. "We of the western world often forget," he wrote, "that many of the most cherished precepts and ideals of our Christian culture come to us from the Hebrews." Then, seeming to attack and judge, Fritsch continued, "It is a shame, however, that the author is utterly blind to some of the most significant contributions of the OT to the development of western culture."

Remarkably, in these two sentences Fritsch kept Jews and Jewish culture invisible to an implied reader for whom the ideals of *Christian* culture were presumed to join seamlessly with the notion of *Western* civilization. However, the unseen of the book review soon appeared. Explicitly identifying

---

only noted philological problems in Jeremias's argument, but voiced suspicion of its ideological subtext.

64. Ithaca: Cornell University Press, 1954. The review appeared in *Journal of Biblical Literature* 74 (1955): 137–38.

Orlinsky as a Jewish professor of Bible at the Hebrew Union College, Fritsch accused him of providing "misinformation" to unwary students, engaging in "pseudo-scientific scholarship," and inflicting his readers with "deadening historicism." Layered beneath the personalized attack was another, more implicit, transgression: Orlinsky had failed to locate certain Christian values and theological ideas, as taproot to stem, deep within the thought world of ancient Israel.

The trouble was, yet again, that Orlinsky tried to separate rigorous historical inquiry from subsequent and contemporary theological reflection. He wanted to keep apart what Fritsch and many other Christian scholars at the time, including the Albrighteans, thought naturally belonged together. While admiring the Bible's religious values and acknowledging its role in shaping democratic societies and three religions of the Western world (arguably a form of cultural, if not theological, valorization of the Bible), Orlinsky nevertheless sought to describe the history of ancient Israel and its religion without, as he wrote, appropriating the Bible's tendency "to interpret all historical experiences as manifestations of divine intervention." Those who created the Bible believed that they had got the truth from a God who entered into a covenant with Israel, but a contemporary historian should not reconstruct biblical history as though he believed it as well. Rather, he "must seek—behind the religious terminology—the same kind of documented human history, with an examination of its underlying dynamics, that would be his proper objective in any other field."[65]

In his book, Orlinsky did not always maintain a clear distinction between *affirming* Israel's faith and *describing* it as belonging to an ancient people. Moreover, from a late twentieth-century perspective, it is possible to question his assumption that the historical objectivity for which he strove could be attained, or that he was any less constrained by socially rooted interests than a theologically oriented Christian scholar. Yet, given his stated view, it might have been reasonable to read Orlinsky's work with a qualifier such as "in the view of the biblical writers" constantly in mind.[66]

Fritsch, however, simply refused Orlinsky his premise, and discussed his differences with Orlinsky not in terms of their conflicting foundational assumptions, but as a matter of accuracy in objectivist historical description. He affixed a label of "misinformation," for example, to Orlinsky's claim that the idea of "messiah" as a superhuman figure was a postbiblical development

65. *Ancient Israel*, 8–9.
66. See *Ancient Israel*, 43.

among Christians and Jews. For Orlinsky, this specific connotation of Hebrew *mashiach* could only "improperly," that is, against the rules of historical method, be attributed to pre-Christian and prerabbinic biblical prophets.

Although this assertion may seem to many rather uncontroversial today, to Fritsch it was outrageous, if not exactly for the reasons he stated. Because it encoded a commitment to historicism without allegiance to contemporary Christian theology, this particular claim about the ancients' messianic belief struck at a Christian affirmation that had been similarly built into the language of Christian historical/theological scholarship. In many and varied ways, it was routinely assumed, the "Old Testament" in some sense prefigured Christ, the Messiah of the "New Testament." The notion had its origins in premodern times, and was already expressed in the evangelists' habit of seeing Hebrew prophecies fulfilled in the events of Jesus' life (e.g., Matthew 1:22–23). When investigating the Bible by the rules of modern historical "science," however, such traditional Christian theological claims posed a difficulty, for they assumed that those particular prophetic words somehow transcended the naturally limited *historical* situation in which they were uttered, and truly referred to a time far distant in the future. How might the traditional prophecy-fulfillment idea be affirmed then, with good modernistic conscience, that is, in language consistent with historically minded people?

One way was to assert, through the language of historical construction, that authentic (religiously true) understandings of Jesus were rooted, not simply in the way early Christians *read* the "Old Testament" prophets, but in the historically situated meanings of the prophets' words themselves when uttered several centuries before Christ. Could this matter have influenced Fritsch, who implied against Orlinsky that the prophets somehow already gave superhuman dimension to the idea of messiah? And could Orlinsky have made his claim, unconsciously perhaps, as ideologically shaped challenge to a long tradition of Christian interpretation?

In any case, Orlinsky was enraged because of what he took as Fritsch's religious polemics and personal attacks. Orlinsky immediately wrote David Noel Freedman, who was editor of the *Journal of Biblical Literature*, but who in his previous role as Old Testament book review editor had assigned to Fritsch the task of reviewing Orlinsky's book. Orlinsky demanded an opportunity for public rebuttal. He never got it, perhaps in part because differences with Albright over the dating and value of the Dead Sea Scrolls (they had become a focus of intense research since their discovery in 1948) had diminished Orlinsky in the eyes of the Albrighteans.

"I resent," wrote Orlinsky, "that a fundamentalist Christian . . . a less than first- or second-rate person, whom you recognized beforehand as hardly competent or reasonably objective, was asked to review the book in America's leading biblical organ." He went on to say that some of his friends had suggested that "some people" (meaning Ernest Wright, Freedman, perhaps even Albright) were trying to "kill the book" because it was not "acceptable Christologically." He preferred not to think that way, he added. "A few people, such as Albright, consider Chap. VII ["The Hebraic Spirit"] of *Ancient Israel* to be a 'Jewish' interpretation." Orlinsky considered that to be untrue, since "liberal Judaism" had not received his interpretation with equanimity. His was a "scholarly attempt to understand what the biblical writers themselves believed and said. If I am wrong, then I am wrong as a scholar, not as a Jew."[67]

Freedman gave his account of the incident to Albright, reporting the "highly personal and vituperative fashion" of Orlinsky's letter, and noting that "he did not scruple to pass on a charge at the whole Baltimore school of trying to 'kill' his book, because it was not 'Christologically' acceptable (whatever that may mean)." Freedman added that he took responsibility for choosing the reviewer, "though denying that Fritsch is a 'fundamentalist' (Harry slings technical Christian terms around very loosely)."[68]

Albright had already written to Freedman on the matter. He faulted Orlinsky on the one hand for *sounding* as though he were anti-theological, and on the other, implied that Orlinsky had *rejected* theology altogether. "I pointed out [to Orlinsky] that one can't take such an ostensibly anti-religious stand without having violent reaction and that the [printed] review was much milder than it was originally."[69]

In comments to Orlinsky, Albright tried to take a mediating position. He defended Freedman ("one must learn by experience as an editor") and Fritsch ("he is not a fundamentalist by any stretch of the imagination"). Albright acknowledged that Fritsch had not been exactly fair to Orlinsky, but at the same time, "your own treatment makes assumptions which most members of SBL [Society of Biblical Literature] cannot accept." Orlinsky should not have dismissed theology, Albright said, and he might have made clearer that he was not ruling out a theological approach but presenting

---

67. Orlinsky to Freedman, copy to Albright, July 24, 1955.
68. Freedman to Albright, August 5, 1955. John Huddlestun informed me that Fritsch had taught Freedman Hebrew at the Princeton Theological Seminary more than a decade earlier.
69. Albright to Freedman, August 1, 1955.

instead a strictly historical interpretation. "I could only call your approach *a* Jewish one," Albright added. "If I had called it agnostic or anti-religious you would have been justly indignant, but that is exactly what it sounded like."[70]

In reply, Orlinsky exposed, but did not quite articulate, the ideological divide. "I am not sure that I can agree with you that *Ancient Israel* is 'agnostic or anti-religious,' merely because it tries to be strictly historical. Would you say that Toynbee is agnostic or anti-religious merely because he tries to describe and account for man's career on earth without saying anywhere in his *Study of History* that God did this and that and everything?"[71]

The suppressed issue was that Orlinsky's refusal of the alliance between historical research and *any* theological construction challenged the normative status that Albright, Freedman, Fritsch, and many others so easily gave to this selfsame alliance. In his mix of assertion and implication, evenhandedness and bias, Albright seemed to exercise the power of that norm by invoking the cloak of a profession that thought of itself, like America, as naturally Christian; anything else was, by suggestion, associated with the antireligious, or agnostic, or simply "a Jewish interpretation." Is it possible that Albright's string of associations permitted a faint smell of anti-Jewish caricature to arise—the Jew who has, or can have, no *real* religion?

If so, one could hardly find a more classic example of ambiguity and ambivalence conspiring to define Orlinsky, the Jew, as outsider. In this perspective, Orlinsky had offended the majority ("most members of SBL") by challenging a pillar in its hegemonic ideology, the joining of historical method with (Christian) theology. And so Albright had reminded Orlinsky of his status as minority, even echoing Freedman's correction of Orlinsky's outsiderlike mistake about the technical meaning of "fundamentalist." Orlinsky had implicitly challenged the intellectual basis of historicotheological biblical study as practiced by most Christian scholars of the time, and from which Albright's "background" approach to the Bible drew its strength among the more conservative members of the profession and Christian churches. From a position of presumed majoritarian rule, his book "sounded agnostic or anti-religious," that is, out of step with the claimed center, the Society of Biblical Literature.[72]

---

70. Albright to Orlinsky, July 29, 1955.

71. Orlinsky to Albright, August 10, 1955.

72. By the time of this exchange, Orlinsky was increasingly at odds with the Albrighteans because of his reluctance to agree with Albright's assessment of the significance of the newly discovered Dead Sea scrolls for sorting out variants in the Hebrew text of the Bible. This particular scholarly debate involved not only Albright's science of typology, which was widely accepted, especially among his students, but ideological conflict as well. Orlinsky doubted the

Irreconcilable Difference

Knowing of this later controversy, it is more understandable that Orlinsky's presence in planning for a theological dictionary a decade earlier would have begun to expose lines of uneasy ideological divide. Perhaps adapting to the direction in which the lexicon had evolved, Orlinsky finally accepted that if the dictionary were to be "theological," then it must treat theological concepts as *ancient* notions held by *ancient* people. He apparently was leery of Hebrew word meanings possibly shaped by, or for, contemporary belief and practice, Christian *or* Jewish.

"I see no need to include the word 'Theological' in the title of the Lexicon," he wrote to Albright. "Any Lexicon of Biblical Hebrew includes the usage of the words, and that means theological. The lexicon is fundamentally linguistic; it has to be."[73] Given that premise, the difficulties over editorship of the volume seemed puzzling. He had been told of Wright's discussions with Trinterud about "credit," and he was convinced that he and Wright would get along. Yet, "the bulk of the work, as Ernest and I saw it, is necessarily linguistic, and will be done by me, with the other editors always reading my material critically, as I would be reading theirs. But I fail to comprehend the necessity of putting Ernest in the position of Editor-in-Chief of the work."

It mattered how Orlinsky was going to be listed on the title page. According to Wright, Trinterud had spoken in terms of readership and marketing—the dictionary should be distinctly theological, unique in the marketplace, with a Christian theologically interested scholar at the head and prominently displayed. Wright talked about credit and fair recognition of responsibilities; both he and Albright spoke of needing Orlinsky's linguistic competence. Yet Orlinsky, though he had told Albright he wasn't concerned about "who will get credit for what," seems finally to have cared. Perhaps also worried about compromising his historicist principles, he questioned the word "Theological" in the title.

The title page, it seems, had become a site of struggle which, besides personal elements, involved ideologies in conflict. I am suggesting the decisions about the title page would not be simply based on private preferences, or on

---

"scientific" value of Albright's classifying scribal handwriting characteristics as datable "types"; Albright used these "typologies," and especially the scrolls, to support his inclination to accept the existing medieval manuscripts of the Hebrew Bible as more reliable than many text critics often thought. See the exchanges between Albright and Orlinsky, e.g., November 18, 22, 28, 1949, and December 11, 19, 22, and 27, 1949; Rabbi Ernst Conrad to Albright, December 22, 1955, and Albright to Conrad, January 3, 1956; Albright to Freedman, December 5, 1955.

73. Harry Orlinsky to Albright, January 4, 1946.

some reputedly pure (abstract, objective) principle. They would be choices rooted in the ambiguities of social processes, in the networks of personal values and ideological commitments with their attendant inclusions and exclusions that helped define relations between the makers and consumers of knowledge about the Bible.

It is well to recall that at midcentury Albright was taken by many as the authoritative center of a network of scholars, some of whom he had trained and subsequently recommended for their teaching posts. As director of the American School of Oriental Research in Jerusalem from 1920 to 1929 (the longest term ever served), and as editor of the *Bulletin of the American Schools of Oriental Research* (he would hold this position well into the 1960s), Albright had put his personal stamp on much of the research, debate, and consensus building by several generations of biblical archaeologists.[74] Because he was an indefatigable lecturer before college, seminary, church, synagogue, and other audiences throughout the country, he and his "backgrounds approach" to building confidence in the Bible also were popular among members of the general public, especially Christians and Jews of traditional or conservative inclinations.[75]

By the early postwar years, it will be remembered, Ernest Wright had rapidly emerged as a second-generation leader in biblical archaeology and energetic promoter of Albrightean perspectives—to other scholars, his own students, and, through the pages of *Biblical Archaeologist*, to a broader public. He was now becoming known as a leader in what would later be called the "biblical theology movement."[76]

Thus the planned theological dictionary, emblazoned with title and headliner names, would present itself, like all such generation-spanning compendiums, as an authoritative statement of reliable knowledge. It would be the best and latest that biblical scholars, especially those associated with Wright and Albright, had to offer. But whose notion of biblical "science" and lexicography was finally to be inscribed as normative for the readers of this reference work?

74. See Philip J. King, *American Archaeology in the Mideast: A History of the American Schools of Oriental Research* (Philadelphia: American Schools of Oriental Research, 1983), esp. 61–84; Delbert Hillers, "Fifty Years of the Bulletin of the American Schools of Oriental Research," *BASOR* 200 (December 1970): 3–7. About Albright's service as editor, Hillers wrote (p. 5), "One may fairly say that over these long years the BULLETIN became very much Dr. Albright's own, a reflection of his interests and judgment."

75. Albright's files of correspondence attest amply to these activities.

76. See King, *American Archaeology*, 106–8, and notes 23 and 57 above.

In theory, Albright and Wright perhaps could grant legitimacy to a secularist historical study of the Bible. But in practice, they thought such approaches in some objective sense to be wrong, misleading, and inadequate. The dictionary, clearly conceived as a linguistic update of the antiquated "BDB,"[77] was also to express an unacknowledged voice of totalizing privilege. It would announce what Wright presumed, the natural join of objectivist, historical biblical study with theological interest in the form of descriptive biblical theology.

A few years later, just after he had convened the first Biblical Colloquium to take up "seize-the-future" projects, Wright would assess the state of Old Testament studies and, among other things, urgently insist that BDB be replaced. Wright would extoll scholars' recovery of *Christian* theological fervor after years of misguided and antiquarian investigation of the Bible's religion, rather than its timeless religious significance; he would lament what seemed to him inherent shortcomings of BDB and would finally project the seemingly incontrovertible need for a different (he implies "adequate") dictionary altogether:

> Yet the advances in our knowledge have been so tremendous that this work is woefully out of date. Furthermore, it was never really adequate. Driver's long articles on the prepositions are excellent, but if one desires to be taught about those things for which the Old Testament exists, he is left to his own devices. The preposition "on, upon" is described in fourteen columns of text, while "righteousness" is given less than four, "justice, judgment" receives two, and "love" one and a half. It is small wonder that the study of Hebrew by theological students is thought to be a waste of time by the vast majority of American clergy. Unless Old Testament scholars can do better than they have done in the past in providing basic tools geared both to the subject matter and needs of the Church, they can expect nothing but an even greater diminution of interest in serious Biblical study.[78]

77. Brown, Driver, and Briggs, eds., *A Hebrew and English Lexicon of the Old Testament* (Oxford: Clarendon Press, 1907).

78. G. Ernest Wright, "The Study of the Old Testament," in Arnold Nash, ed., *Protestant Thought in the Twentieth Century: Whence & Whither?* (New York: Macmillan, 1951), 40. See pp. 22–23, where Wright spelled out the "tragedy" of Protestant biblical study as a "neutral science, largely separated from any responsible feeling for the on-going life of the churches." Planning for the Westminster theological lexicon had been suspended when Wright wrote this essay. In

I suggest that Orlinsky's insistence on "credit" and his fixation on the title exposed ambiguities that had so far masked conceptual conflicts between different worlds of linguistic practice among biblical scholars. His persistent reservations cracked open the veneered working conditions of Christian and Jew as each set about studying according to a commonly held method what was thought to be the same Bible. His dogged pursuit of questions makes visible the opposed notions about what counted for biblical studies, despite the common allegiance to assumptions of scientific inquiry. Clashes over the title of the book and recognition of its contributors point toward that place where the discourse of biblical scholars practicing their craft jostled formations of social power that were assumed, defended, or opposed.

Albright did not reply right away to Orlinsky's complaint about "Theological" in the title, and about Wright having to be "Editor-in-Chief." This fact would not ordinarily be notable, except for the evidence that Albright and Wright were very carefully considering how best to deal with Orlinsky's challenge, perhaps without fundamentally altering the situation. Albright drafted a letter which was later inscribed in his sprawling script: "First draft, read by Ernest and cancelled."[79] The letter he actually sent was considerably shorter.

In the draft, a friendly and gracious Albright emerges out of chitchat about settling in to a term as visitor at the Oriental Institute in Chicago. Blended with such pleasantries, Albright mentioned visits to relatives, one of whom was a cousin who married a Jewish man and converted to Judaism, "which is very nice and will give me an excellent chance to accent my philo-Semitism."

The remark seems curious. Albright was indeed philo-Semitic. But why would he have been moved to mention this feeling, least of all to Orlinsky, with whom he had worked closely for several years? Albright was greatly admired by Jews, and in the 1940s he was widely known as an outspoken Zionist.[80] Is it possible that Trinterud's excluded Jew returns in this document, but only dimly reflected in Albright's rhetoric of philo-Semitic credentials?

---

this same book, Floyd Filson, who was also involved in planning the Westminster dictionary, made similar pleas: "A lexicon of the Greek Old Testament, and a new lexicon of the Greek New Testament, are urgent needs. They should give major attention to the theological usage of the words" (65 n. 38).

79. Albright to Orlinsky (draft), January 17, 1946.

80. Albright's pro-Zionist activities have not been chronicled, but they were extensive during the 1940s, and are fully documented in his files of correspondence. See also Running and Freedman, *Albright*, 374–90.

In any case, Albright went on to explain that the lexicon was not like the original Hebrew-English Dictionary, "for which Trinterud was unable to find support." He was, however, able to secure backing for a theological work, so naturally plans had to change. Even though Wright does not like the new setup, Albright said, and even though he argued long and hard, Trinterud remains adamant because his publication board insists on a theological dictionary with a "Presbyterian Editor-in-Chief." He hoped Orlinsky could agree. Seeming now to distance himself even further from the dispute, Albright wrote that in the event of continuing disagreement, that Orlinsky explain his reasons to Trinterud (Orlinsky had been communicating only with Wright and Albright), so that Trinterud in turn would be able to carry the matter directly to "his board." Disavowing sectarian bias, Albright finally assured Orlinsky that as long as Ernest was in "nominal charge," he and the others on the committee would guarantee a scholarly, not dogmatic, approach to theological definitions.

The letter that Albright actually sent to Orlinsky included a more intimate description of the Jewish cousin, deleted the explicit reference to "philo-Semitism," and offered a briefer account of the dictionary. Mentioning that the project had become a "Theological Dictionary of the Old Testament," since Trinterud could not secure the backing of his board for the original concept, Albright stated that Wright had been arguing for some time with Trinterud about organizational details. He hoped that Orlinsky would go along "in spite of some not quite satisfactory elements in the set-up, since Wright, Burrows and I will see to it that there is a scholarly, not a dogmatic approach to theological treatment of individual words."[81]

This version of events is notable both for its lack of detail and for its appeal to misleading impressions. Notably, Trinterud's pointed strictures against Orlinsky, "or any Jew," remain unspoken. (In the draft, perhaps reflecting ambiguities in various conversations on the matter, Albright had turned the privately stated requirement for a *Christian* editor in chief into "Presbyterian," as though it were a matter of denominational pride at a Presbyterian publishing house.) Moreover, all the difficulties with planning I have discussed do not appear to be implicit in the sketchy narrative of changed design. Some may have been. Missing, however, are Wright's (and Trinterud's) growing excitement about biblical theology, which may have overtaken the original idea of a merely philological dictionary, and Albright's interested support for the advancement of his own "background" approach

81. Albright to Orlinsky, January 19, 1946.

to biblical research. Albright also had hoped that the Westminster Press and the Presbyterians would popularize a more conservative, or "neo-orthodox" use of the Bible. Just a few months before writing this letter to Orlinsky, Albright considered this emergent possibility. "Trinterud is in the process of revolutionizing American religious publication," he wrote to Walther Eichrodt, whose theological work, it may be recalled, Albright thought would make a solid base for the new dictionary. "Neo-orthodoxy is now best exemplified by the Presbyterians, and the Westminster Press is the best suited press in the country to launch an elaborate publication program."[82]

It is striking that barely three months after writing these words about religious renewal, Albright construed himself and Wright as somewhat powerless in the matter of the dictionary. Perhaps their power was limited—after all, they were not the publishers and marketers of the work. Yet Albright permitted the inference that they, and even Trinterud, had to submit to a distant "board" which insisted on a different project, a shift from linguistic to theological focus, as the price for its "support." He seemed to imply, especially in the unposted draft, that everyone had been forced to compromise. One may wonder, however, what exactly Wright, and Albright for that matter, had given up, except their desire to recognize more fairly Orlinsky's responsibilities in this theological dictionary.

Meanwhile, Orlinsky conceded one point and pressed another. "I do not see the need for beating about the bush about the appearance of the title page," he wrote to Albright. "Since the Theology is now as important as the Philology, what stands in the way of having the Dictionary 'Edited by' the two of us, 'with the cooperation of' the Britisher?"[83]

Albright's reply was noncommittal. A meeting among the editors had not yet taken place, he said, so "the Hebrew Dictionary plans are still very much up in the air. I have been dragged in tentatively, as you probably know, but we are not really any farther along than before."[84] Further discussions must have taken place, for a few weeks later Orlinsky concluded that even this level of visibility for him on the title page met with adamant resistance. (His objections, perhaps unawares, went against the policy settled on by the lexicon committee, that each volume have a single general editor.) It was

82. Albright to Walther Eichrodt, October 3, 1945.

83. Orlinsky to Albright, February 10, 1946. Trinterud and the editorial committee had thought it advisable to include a British scholar as one of the "associate editors," partly to help secure a co-publishing arrangement with a British firm, and partly to head off any rival publication that might be proposed in Great Britain.

84. Albright to Orlinsky, March 2, 1946.

then, in March of 1946, that Orlinsky withdrew from the project and stated his belief that Trinterud and the Westminster Press had sought to hire his scholarship and "suppress the Jewishness of the scholar on the title page."

Albright wrote him a conciliatory letter, but avoided Orlinsky's allusion to the suppressed Jew of Christian Hebraists. "I don't blame you in the least for being disgusted and quitting," he said. Expressing his disappointment, Albright explained the situation again, and once more obscured the issues that coalesced around "editor" and effaced his own investment in the project as it had evolved toward theologically vested exegesis, that is, toward what both Wright and Albright implicitly accepted as a normative model of biblical studies. Trinterud had failed to win support for a philological dictionary (under Orlinsky's editorship Albright said). However, a new opportunity had presented itself—Albright suggested that it was fortuitous—in connection with an English handbook of theological terms, presumably in New Testament Greek, linked to Wright's colleague, Floyd Filson. "A Hebrew section was included," said Albright. "Wright and you were to edit that, together with an unnamed Englishman." In view of Orlinsky's resignation, Albright continued, he had been forced to take responsibility for the Hebrew portions of the new project. He did not want the job and was "manoeuvred" [*sic*] into the position, but hoped to get "younger men to carry the main burden."[85]

It is reasonable to think that Wright and Albright were caught in an emotional squeeze between Trinterud's demands, enthusiasm for Christian biblical theology, respect for Orlinsky, and need for his skills as a Semiticist. I do not minimize the difficulties they faced in attempting to maintain conflicting commitments, especially since at the time these were not always clear or even articulated. Nevertheless, as events unfolded Wright and Albright were able to employ the power they and the Westminster Press held to define what counted for critical practice in the study of the Bible, and to codify that practice in a major publication.

It appears that they were never directly challenged to dilute that power by redirecting it to a differently conceived project. This one, after all, was the one that the Westminster Press and the theologically vested Ernest Wright were supporting. The structure of the negotiations may also have worked against a deviation from the plan. It appears that Trinterud and Orlinsky did not deal directly with each another. Prior associations and membership on the official editorial committee gave to Albright and Wright an insider's

85. Albright to Orlinsky, March 29, 1946.

path to Trinterud, and a sense of protocol caused Orlinsky, apparently, to communicate only with Wright and Albright. They in turn represented Trinterud to Orlinsky while mediating Orlinsky's voice back to Trinterud and other members inside the editorial circle. The fuller dimensions of the situation that I have enticed from the record could be kept from Orlinsky, and perhaps even from themselves, as the language of diplomacy and avoidance effaced ideological conflict. I see no suggestion that Orlinsky felt that either Wright or Albright shared any responsibility in the outcome. Perhaps to suggest "responsibility" is to use too strong a word. It is sufficient to note the web of commitments and interests that came together, were played out in concrete actions, and were honored in the complicated manipulation of what was presented.

In any case, planning for the dictionary was hardly disrupted by Orlinsky's resignation. There even seemed to be some relief. When Albright wrote his conciliatory words to Orlinsky, suggesting politely that "perhaps we can induce you later to come in again in an advisory capacity,"[86] he had already accepted more direct responsibility in the project. The day before writing Orlinsky, Albright outlined to Wright his plans to hire two of his own students as dictionary workers. Both were Protestant Christians then studying at Johns Hopkins University; they would hardly refuse the job or pose the same challenges as Orlinsky. Besides, these new members of the team were unambiguously sons, or rather, grandsons, of Albright. One, George Mendenhall, had been led to Albright by Jacob Myers, his teacher at Gettysburg Theological Seminary; the other, Frank Moore Cross, Jr., had been so prepared by Ernest Wright for graduate studies that many years later David Noel Freedman would recall that when Cross arrived at Hopkins, he "knew more about Albright and about what was going on than *I* did after I had been there a year."[87]

"With Mendenhall and Cross, you and I can rest easy," Albright wrote. "We really have able—even brilliant—young men who can carry the bulk of the work and who will not be so hard to work with as Harry might be."[88] Ironically, the very next day he expressed the same hopes to Orlinsky, freely giving to others what had been, for Orlinsky, greatly encumbered: "I hope to get younger men to carry the main burden, in return for compensation and inclusion on the title page."[89]

86. Idem.
87. Running and Freedman, *Albright*, 216.
88. Albright to Wright, March 28, 1946.
89. Albright to Orlinsky, March 29, 1946.

Despite all this new optimism, however, within three months Albright reported that in light of Trinterud's resignation from his position at the Press, the project was "extinct."[90] Nevertheless, Albright and Wright were determined to carry on, and in the theological mode that had evolved. Apparently neither Albright nor Wright considered returning to a conventional Hebrew dictionary of the sort that, according to Albright's statement, Trinterud and his "board" had opposed. This fact alone suggests again the stake they both, and especially Wright, had in the basic theological, rather than philological, design of the project.

Wright immediately began courting the Lutheran Board of Publication for support (Mendenhall, one of Albright's "younger men," was a Lutheran clergyman and Albright had earlier pleased the Lutherans with what he called a piece of "theological apologetics" in one of their publications).[91] Wright set Frank Moore Cross, Jr., to work on compiling a list of theological words so that Wright himself could draft a "few trial entries for the lexicon."[92] By January of 1947 he was "desperately" trying to clear the slate so as to "spend the whole summer beginning work on that lexicon." Wright even wanted to move the project to Johns Hopkins under the mentoring eye of Albright, adding, "It is the most important single project in the O.T. field that I know of at the moment."[93] Some five years later, Wright would be using annual meetings of the Biblical Colloquium to present studies of theological words slated for the dictionary.[94] Remarkably, a student at Harvard from the 1960s testified that Wright was singling out promising graduate students to write articles destined for the dictionary.[95]

The lexicon, however, was never published. Another firm could not be persuaded to take up the task, and Wright's hopes that the Colloquium could provide the technical labor force never quite materialized. Members simply developed other interests, and collectively they found other venues for planting and reaping the fruits of Albrightean researches. By the mid-1950s, the sons and grandsons of Albright were planning the much grander

---

90. Albright to Orlinsky, June 22, 1946. Trinterud had become embroiled in some internal dispute at the Press, and had resigned his position as religious book editor. Wright to Albright, April 13, 1947.

91. Wright to Albright, October 23, 1946.

92. Wright to Albright, November 28, 1946.

93. Wright to Albright, January 6, 1947. More elaborate plans were mentioned in Wright's letter to Albright, April 13, 1947.

94. Cross to Albright, December 3, 1952.

95. Interview with a graduate of the Harvard program in Near Eastern Languages and Civilizations, 1994.

and different, but in some ways successor, project, the multivolumed *Anchor Bible*. Then, in 1961, James Barr published his devastating critique of the lexicographical premises that undergirded the then-conventional thinking about studies of theological words.[96] Soon after that, the matter seemed to be laid finally to rest.

The Wright-Albright-Trinterud dictionary, however, remains an instructive episode in the history of the Albright school at midcentury. In one of its many layers, the project was a matter of enlisting a Jew's philological expertise in a Christian project. Associations between this division of labor and patterns deeply rooted in the history of Christian Hebraism could not be entirely suppressed as it turned out, despite faith that methods of historical study of the Bible created a space free of the legacies of such Christian hegemony. Yet, Orlinsky's angry outburst named only one layer of the complex social realities he and others perceived. To Trinterud, the project *was* a Christian one, aimed at Christian readers, with Christian interests at heart and, I would think, inseparable from his perception of Albright as a kind of fellow evangelist, "thrusting into the whole of American biblical literature a more scholarly and positive interpretation of the Christian Gospel."[97] Thus, the needs and ambitious desires, even social power, of a sectarian publisher, a seller of books, fell together with another set of exclusions, the evangelization of America. And for Albright and Wright, this effort fit comfortably with their own theological interests, although they might not have expressed them with such old-fashioned-sounding piety. Historical study of the Bible yoked to the interests of Christian theology and religious practice, even if not narrowly sectarian, was the presumed "natural" way of most scholars during the postwar years. The Albrighteans gave it their particular stamp, tying advances in gaining theological truth and revitalizing the Bible to the results of ever-refined archaeological explorations into the background of the Bible.

96. James Barr, *The Semantics of Biblical Language* (London: Oxford University Press, 1961). Among other things, Barr raised serious questions about a book edited by Gerhard Kittel, *Theologisches Wörterbuch des Neuen Testament* (Stuttgart: Kohlhammer, from 1933 = *Theological Dictionary of the New Testament*, trans. Geoffrey Bromiley (Grand Rapids: Eerdmans, 1964–74). "Kittel" had apparently been a model for what Trinterud and Wright had in mind. It would be 1970 before a similarly massive undertaking for the Hebrew Bible would be published, and with premises somewhat altered by post–James Barr discussions of linguistic matters. See G. Johannes Botterweck and Helmer Ringren, *Theologisches Wörterbuch zum Alten Testament* (Stuttgart: Kohlhammer, 1970–). An English translation is now appearing as *Theological Dictionary of the Old Testament* (Grand Rapids: Eerdmans, 1974–).

97. Trinterud to Albright, January 19, 1945.

Orlinsky apparently thought he could be free of such apologetics (in hindsight, one may question his naïveté). His presence on the team began to suggest that the Albrighteans' privileged assumptions were less natural and more a matter of preference and commitment than the Christian scholars may have supposed. The question of Orlinsky's name on the title page of the book nearly forced this issue to the surface. Albright and Wright stumbled over their ambivalence when the Jew, perhaps unrecognized as alien but nevertheless having been implicitly defined as such, required his recognition and, concomitantly, demanded commitment to ideological assumptions different from those held by the Christian scholars.

This challenge from the margins, from one who in the end had to be pushed to the edge of the Albrightean (Christian) theological/historical practice, finally came to nothing. Albright and Wright maintained their privileged dominance (they were after all perceived as aligned fully with Trinterud's desires), and the power of their normativeness held firm. Change did not occur, or the incipient oppositional discourse gained no lasting space, and therefore no social power or recognition.

Orlinsky never seemed to realize the social and ideological complexity that, for me, makes this incident into a multiply enfolded thing. He remained cordial and generous toward Albright and Wright in the aftermath of his resignation. But the will-to-dominance, which was to be much more in evidence during activities of the Biblical Colloquium, was already clear enough, at least from the perspective of our day when challenges to all manner of canonized authority are becoming one mark of critical reflection.

4　FICTIVE SELF
The Power of Mythic Image in Biblical Archaeology

In providing historical context for the Wright-Filson-Albright theological dictionary and activities directly related to Wright's Biblical Colloquium, I noted how certain implied narratives set paradigms for Albright and his sons to shape not only their scholarly research, but a patriarchally ordered culture of generational and ideological solidarity. Albright's myth of supplantation, the narrative of a dawning era in biblical studies, was of central importance, and it represented oppositional voices as antagonists on a landscape undergoing radical and progressive change. Since Albright and many of his students, at least in the two decades following World War II, yoked their activities to Christian theological purpose, conflict with non-Christian ideologies, even if largely repressed, was inevitable. In planning for the dictionary, and the *Anchor Bible*, these ambiguities in Jewish-Christian relations surfaced in ways that pushed the Albrighteans to define ever more precisely the borders of their inner circle.

In discussing these particular dynamics, I often alluded to principles and values of modern scientific inquiry that formed part of the complicated mix of Albright's ideological commitments. As the planters and reapers of Albright enacted their teacher's myth of supplantation, they might also be understood as living another, perhaps equally powerful paradigm, a narrative of iterative scientific discovery.

When he was fifty-seven years old, Albright wrote that his move to Jerusalem nearly three decades earlier, and the discoveries he made while anchored in that city, were decisive in defining his attitude toward the

Bible. An "initially rather skeptical attitude toward the accuracy of Israelite historical tradition," he recalled, "had suffered repeated jolts as discovery after discovery confirmed the historicity of details which might reasonably have been considered legendary." These same discoveries intensified his opposition to Julius Wellhausen's outline of Israelite religious history, and led him "increasingly to insist on the substantial historicity of the Mosaic tradition and the antiquity of Israelite monotheism."[1]

When I first encountered this figure of speech—a passage from skepticism to conviction—I was struck immediately by its imaginative appeal. From that point, I embarked on a journey through the byways of what might be called the mythification of self, which in turn opened onto Albright's embrace of a scientific culture that was widely acclaimed, popularized, and lionized in early twentieth-century America. I came to consider the power of configured self to shape academic discourse, in Albright's case biblical archaeology, which perhaps more than any other field of biblical criticism carries the legacy of his formidable contributions.

It is testimony to Albright's remarkably powerful presence as well as to the attractiveness of this particular metaphor, that several writers regularly repeated the phrase, or at least its sense, when assessing and paying homage to Albright. His biographers reported that Albright "remembered how 'liberal' he had become during his university studies." He thought he might have remained so persuaded had not topographical and archaeological work continually confirmed biblical tradition.[2] A historian of the American Schools of Oriental Research transmuted that recollection into settled fact:

> As a young man Albright shared the skepticism of his mentor Haupt about the historical value of the biblical traditions. In time, however, he became more conservative and repudiated the radical views of Haupt. Archaeology provided the external evidence that led Albright and others to a more positive attitude about the early traditions of Israel.[3]

1. Louis Finkelstein, ed., *American Spiritual Autobiographies* (New York: Harper & Brothers, 1948), 165.

2. Running and Freedman, *Albright*, 109. See also John A. Miles, Jr., "Understanding Albright: A Revolutionary Etude," *Harvard Theological Review* 69 (1976): 151–75, especially p. 152: "He [Albright] first came upon anomalous archaeological evidence and made the necessary, drastic revision of the synthesis of biblical history reached by the 'higher criticism' of the nineteenth century."

3. Philip King, *American Archaeology in the Mideast: A History of the American Schools of Oriental Research* (Philadelphia: American Schools of Oriental Research, 1983), 52.

Albright's own view, and in virtually his own words, was even passed along to the National Academy of Science in support of his nomination to membership in 1956.[4]

John Bright, a student from the 1930s, it will be recalled, ventured and argued a similar point. Albright generally thought the Bible preserved reliable history, but, Bright assured his readers, his teacher had not come to this view because of "dogmatic presuppositions as some have seemed to think (he rigidly adhered to the historico-critical method), but on the basis of objective external evidence," facts that had been derived from excavations in Mesopotamia and Palestine.[5] Some years later Edward Campbell Jr., a third-generation grandson[6] cited the oral authority of patriarchy:

> He [Albright] asserted regularly that it was the force of evidence, of the data and the warrants for their pertinence, which led him rather rapidly in his first decade in Jerusalem to place a higher degree of confidence in the worth for historical reconstruction of most of what both prose narrative and poetic texts in the Bible contained.[7]

Despite such consensus, should Albright's declaration or its affirmation by others be taken at face value? Acts of recollection, as Freud taught, involve selection, loss, and repression as a past is re-membered out of dismembered experience. From the heights of mid-career, Albright gave his readers a constructed moment from his formative years. What complexities might this artifact hold within its appealing form? And why has its sense proved so plausible that Albright's commentators, Albrightean sons or not, passed it on as canonical text?

4. The printed nomination papers were enclosed in a letter from Edwin B. Wilson to Albright, April 1, 1956.

5. John Bright, "William F. Albright as an Historical and Biblical Scholar," in David Noel Freedman, *The Published Works of William Foxwell Albright: A Comprehensive Bibliography* (Cambridge, Mass.: American Schools of Oriental Research, 1975), 6–7.

6. He had studied with Ernest Wright, then with Albright, and, when Wright went to teach at Harvard, took up his teacher's post at McCormick Seminary.

7. Edward Campbell, Jr., "W. F. Albright and Historical Reconstruction," *Biblical Archaeologist* 42 (1979): 39. Even Albright's own assertion demanded some interpretation, however, and Campbell obliged by stating that the methodological principle involved was a "willingness to admit a *possibility* of historicity in a text" (p. 40; emphasis added). J. Max Miller, in the same article, interpreted Albright's principle not as admission of *possible* historicity, but as a *presumption* that behind a biblical text was an actual event, even if the text itself is a misleading guide to its true nature (p. 42).

Con(re)version

Albright made his way through Egypt to Jerusalem in late 1919, when he was just twenty-eight years old. He was to begin a postgraduate year as the annual Thayer Fellow at the American School. Barely nine months later, in September of 1920, he confessed to Samuel Geiser, a close friend from college days, that "the stand I take on biblical questions is now very conservative and sober, tho [*sic*] this has always been my tendency, as you may remember from the Academia days."[8]

Less than two months later—it was now November of 1920—Albright told James B. Nies that he had "recanted all the more or less novel opinions" drawn from his teacher Paul Haupt and put into his earlier article on the Joseph story.[9] The confession seemed in part calculated for the confessor. An ambitious but cautious Albright described Nies at the time as a "charming old gentleman," a personal "warm friend and backer . . . who always predicts a brilliant orientalistic career for me and will supply me with funds if I run short."[10] He would have been loath to offend Nies, a "great patron of Oriental learning," and a generous benefactor of the Jerusalem school.[11] Albright took care not to burden Nies with untraditional beliefs about the Bible. With detailed letters he kept Nies informed of the latest explorations in Palestine and of their importance to the Bible's historical details and religious ideas.[12] These courtly epistles—they are remarkable for suggesting Albright's admiration for his patron's wealth and socially prominent family—make it clear that both Nies and Albright presumed that the Bible in its general outline and sequencing was to be taken more or less as it announced itself.

8. Albright to Samuel Geiser, September 26, 1920. The title Academia referred to a self-styled "Genius Club" founded by Dr. Daniel Mason Parker at Upper Iowa University, where Albright and Geiser formed a lifelong friendship. See Running and Freedman, *Albright*, 15.

9. Albright to James B. Nies, November 11, 1920. The article was published as "Historical and Mythological Elements in the Joseph Story," *Journal of Biblical Literature* 37 (1918): 111–43.

10. Albright to his mother, Zephine Viola Albright, November 7, 1919. At Paul Haupt's urging, during the very next year Nies supported Albright's candidacy for acting director of the School. Paul Haupt to Albright, May 22, 1920.

11. A. T. Clay, "In Memoriam," *Bulletin of the American Schools of Oriental Research* 7 (October 1922): 2. See Philip King, *American Archaeology*, 66. At about this time, the Jerusalem school had received a $50,000 bequest from the estate of Mrs. Nies.

12. By now, the earlier misgivings that Nies had expressed to Julian Morgenstern about Albright's Haupt-like treatment of the Joseph story had been set aside. Nies to Julian Morgenstern, June 26, 1919 (Julian Morgenstern Papers, American Jewish Archives, Cincinnati, Ohio).

Expanding on his differences with Haupt, Albright explained to Nies the substance of his "new" conservatism:

> The fourteenth chapter of Genesis, the career of Abram, the Exodus, and the Song of Deborah now come at last into a clear historic perspective . . . due largely, I think, to the finally exact results I have obtained in Babylonian chronology, which now agrees exactly with Breasted's Egyptian for the second millennium.[13]

It is difficult to imagine what archaeological facts Albright could have discovered during those first nine months in British Mandate Palestine. What pushed him to reject Hauptian novelty, or jolted him out of his skepticism about the Bible's historical value, or turned him toward what he told Sam Geiser were "conservative and sober" positions? Reporting that "not much could be accomplished in archaeology" owing to bad weather and political problems—it was a time of severe Jewish-Arab tension—Albright concentrated on studies of modern Hebrew and Arabic during his first months in Jerusalem.[14] Furthermore, if a newly established chronology was the key to recanting error, as he had confessed to Nies, it was a key he carried in his pocket when he traveled to Jerusalem.

Albright had actually plotted his new chronology the year before while at the Johns Hopkins University in Baltimore. At a meeting of the American Oriental Society in April 1919, he announced the crucial discovery: a reference point in Egyptian chronology by which to date many other rulers and events in biblical and Near Eastern history.[15] Six months after taking up residence in Jerusalem, and before engaging directly in archaeological

13. Albright to James B. Nies, November 11, 1920. See Running and Freedman, *Albright*, 85–86. The material to which Albright alluded was published shortly thereafter: "A Revision of Early Assyrian and Middle Babylonian Chronology," *Revue d'Assyriologie* 18 (1921): 83–94; "A Revision of Early Hebrew Chronology," *Journal of the Palestine Oriental Society* 1 (1921): 49–79. The latter was read before the Palestine Oriental Society in November 1920 (Running and Freedman, *Albright*, 84).

14. *Bulletin of the American Schools of Oriental Research*. 3 (April 1921): 2. Hereafter, cited as *BASOR*.

15. Albright described the importance of his discovery in a letter to his father written just a few days after arriving in Jerusalem. On the basis of identifying Menes, the first dynastic king of Egypt, with a "Mani of Magan," said to have been defeated by the Babylonian king Naram-Sin, Albright offered a new reconstruction of the dynastic chronology in Egypt coordinated with inscriptions from Mesopotamia. He then arranged undated biblical events, presumed to have occurred more or less as they were reported, within this chronological framework. (Albright to Wilbur Finley Albright, January 11, 1920.) The lecture was later published as "Menes and Naram-Sin," *Journal of Egyptian Archaeology* 6 (1920): 89–98, 295–96.

excavation, the young Albright was still reflecting on the implications of his earlier discovery for confirming a trustworthy Bible, something he knew to be of special interest to his father. At the time, Albright was preparing a few essays for publication. My works "are not of a nature to hurt anybody's faith, the last thing on earth I want to do," he told his mother, adding that in fact he had confirmed rather traditional dates for events and books of the Bible. By successfully coordinating secular with sacred history, he wrote, he could fix the latter's chronology "within a decade." Albright assigned the Israelites' departure from Egypt to 1260 B.C.E., the battle of Tanach, associated with Deborah in the book of Judges, to around 1180, and attributed the composition of Chronicles–Ezra–Nehemiah assuredly to Ezra, within a decade of 420. "All these results are hopelessly conservative in appearance," he added, "even if the treatment is just as incorrigibly and rigidly critical and methodical as ever."[16]

Albright's very conservative and sober tendency, as he had put it to Sam Geiser, joined to "rigidly critical" method, seems to have found a happy metier in Jerusalem. His (pre)disposition, it seems, was deeply congruent with the social and intellectual climate of Jerusalem, and indeed with much of the American public, which hungered after sensational Bible-confirming finds from archaeological excavations. The school's founding scholars, its managing committee, most American professors of Bible who were oriented toward biblical archaeology, and even many Assyriologists made their activities a blend of Protestant Christian piety and humanistic "science." Many had been trained, de rigueur, at venerable German universities, where they had learned the ways of historical and linguistic studies of ancient texts. They returned to North America and applied this scientific approach to the Bible.[17] Not many Jews participated in this biblical science, as criticism was called at the time. Those who did, such as Cyrus Adler and Morris Jastrow (they were members of the American School's executive committee when Albright arrived in Jerusalem), or Max Margolis (he edited the *Journal of Biblical Literature* from 1914 to 1921), or Julian Morgenstern (he had begun his career at the Hebrew Union College in 1907), followed a similar track. They shared the scientific attitude without its specifically Christian expression.

However, the generally accepted mores of the day approved of scholarship that carried within itself a vague religiosity, more sentiment it appears

16. Albright to Zephine Viola Albright, July 19, 1920.
17. King, *American Archaeology*, 25–31.

than dogma. The language of scientific discourse about the Bible served as one important medium of exchange between science and religion. In his 1910 presidential address before the Society of Biblical Literature and Exegesis, Harvard professor David Lyon caught the consensus rather well: "The chief motive which prompts to Palestinian study in all its phases is religious and Biblical. . . . As the tourist goes to that country for religious quickening or for confirmation and elucidation of the Scriptures, so the student is moved by the same motive."[18]

Chairing the executive committee of the American School in its early years, and editing its semipopular *Bulletin*, was James A. Montgomery, an Episcopal clergyman whose father's line of descent included several other Episcopal ministers. Montgomery combined active church work with scholarly pursuits until 1907, when he devoted himself exclusively to teaching, writing, and editing at the Philadelphia Divinity School and the graduate school of the University of Pennsylvania.[19] According to one admiring eulogist, scholarship and theology remained for him a "happy synthesis," as much a mark of his own personality as the field in which he labored.[20]

Under Montgomery's editorship (he would edit the publication until 1930), issues of the *Bulletin* frequently appealed to readers whose interests in the Bible were both devotional and academic. Soon after his arrival as fellow, and then as director of the American School, Albright toured the land making archaeological surveys and contributing a number of essays entirely consistent with such expectations. His reports were one part research account and one part investigative travelogue, generously dashed with extracts from a pilgrim's diary. Combining youthful investigative appetite with romantic piety, Albright told his readers (perhaps with an eye toward soliciting financial support) that:

> these unassuming mounds among the hills of Ephraim and Benjamin are of the greatest interest to us, since they represent authentic

18. David Lyon, "Archaeological Exploration of Palestine," *Journal of Biblical Literature* 30 (1911): 4. One could spy other motivations as well, especially among the national politicians of Europe and America. See Neil Asher Silberman, *Digging for God and Country: Exploration, Archeology, and the Secret Struggle for the Holy Land, 1799–1917* (New York: Alfred A. Knopf, 1982), and *Between Past and Present: Archaeology, Ideology, and Nationalism in the Modern Middle East* (New York: Doubleday, 1989).

19. David Noel Freedman, "Montgomery, James Alan," *Dictionary of American Biography*, Suppl. 4 (New York: Charles Scribner's Sons, 1974), 594–96.

20. Ephraim A. Speiser, "James Alan Montgomery (1866–1949)," *BASOR* 115 (October 1949): 4–8.

monuments of the Israelite past. Every stone and potsherd they conceal is hallowed to us by association with the great names of the Bible. Who can think of the tells which mark ancient Mizpah and Gibeah without a thrill, as memory calls up the shade of Samuel, and the heroic figure of Saul?[21]

Gazing upon another biblical site, Albright wrote of his hopes for future excavations at Ashkelon: "Here will be discoveries to confute the skeptic and delight the scholar's heart, to extend our knowledge of our own past, and to illustrate many a passage of Holy Writ."[22]

Sometimes attached to awakenings of nationalist pride, such sentiments were routinely found in published appeals for financial support of archaeological research. The needs were great in the early 1920s, and since France, Germany, and Great Britain had been weakened by World War I, opportunity beckoned for Americans to assume a more commanding role in exploring western Asia and satisfying their hunger for a romanticized Holy Land. Sounding a bit desperate, Montgomery told his readers:

> If America is to maintain an honorable place in the international plan for archaeological work in Palestine outlined above, an increased income must be obtained at once. All members of the Archaeological Institute [the parent institution of the American School] and all lovers of the Bible are earnestly urged to come to our aid.[23]

In a subsequent issue the appeal became more elaborate—a whole page was devoted to the school's financial plight. Montgomery concluded that "religious, patriotic and scientific motives combine to call loudly for subscriptions to the support of the School."[24]

Similarly, Paul Haupt urgently counseled his pupil and protégé Albright:

> Let me urge you again, hunt for the *Mons Testaceus* at the junction of the valleys of Hinnom, Kidron, and Tyropoean, also for the site of the

---

21. *BASOR* 6 (May 1922): 9.

22. Ibid., 14. See also *BASOR* 4 (1921): 7–11; 9 (February 1923): 8–10. While freely expressing his own devotion to both science and religion, Albright disliked the same in people he thought excessively enthusiastic in defending religious dogma. See *BASOR* 11 (October 1923): 5.

23. *BASOR* 1 (December 1919): 4. Albright apparently shared or took on some of these same values, to judge from his own expression of nationalistic sentiment (*BASOR* 11 [October 1923]: 4; 12 [December 1923]: 11–12).

24. *BASOR* 2 (February 1920): 9.

Inn at Bethlehem referred to in my paper on the Crib of Christ. . . . If you succeed in one of these explorations, funds will be forthcoming for operations on a more extensive scale.[25]

Few, if any, among Albright's new associates in Jerusalem thought differently, save for particularities of religious or national allegiances.[26] Indeed, for the most part, they were part of the consensus that David Lyon had articulated in 1910 before the assembled society of biblical scholars.

Life at the Jerusalem school during 1919–20 would have reflected this mix of traditional piety, scientific attitudes, and national pride. Internal tensions among staff members brought its politics to the surface. On one side were the evangelical zealotry of Albert T. Clay (he was an anti-Zionist) and the quieter traditional piety of John Peters; and on the other side, William Worrell, a pro-Arab liberal Unitarian and an accomplished specialist in Coptic archaeology and languages.[27] Albright tried to maintain public neutrality on the Arab-Jewish issues, but was caught in the middle of abusive personal clashes between Clay and Worrell.[28] During Albright's first year as Thayer fellow, Peters was a lecturer, Worrell was director of the school, and Clay was the annual professor (though he treated Worrell, some thirteen years his junior, as a little-regarded subordinate).

Clay was an influential member of the Jerusalem school's managing committee, and at the time probably the best-known Assyriologist in America. A student of Hilprecht at the University of Pennsylvania (he had received a Ph.D. in 1894), Clay taught at his alma mater for eleven years before assuming the Laffan Professorship of Assyriology at Yale. He held that

25. Paul Haupt to Albright, July 6, 1920. Earlier, Haupt had written, "If you should find Golgotha I am sure it would help you very much, and not only you, but also the [American] School [of Oriental Research]" (Haupt to Albright, May 22, 1920).

26. The most active archaeologists in Palestine in 1920 included Pythian-Adams, associated with John Garstang, a notorious apologist for how diggings in the land confirmed the Bible; Pére Louis H. Vincent; Pére Marie-Joseph Lagrange; Eduard Dhorme; Herbert Danby; Gustav Dalman.

27. After graduating from the University of Michigan, William Hoyt Worrell took a theology degree from the Hartford Theological Seminary in 1906, and then studied comparative Semitics in Germany and France. He received his Ph.D. from the University of Strasbourg in 1909. He taught Semitics at Hartford from 1910 until 1925, when he returned to the University of Michigan as professor of Semitics, a post he held until his retirement in 1949. See *Who Was Who*, vol. 3 (Chicago: Marquis, 1960), 941.

28. See Running and Freedman, *Albright*, 69. Clay accused Worrell of misrepresenting to the managing committee "practically anything I said and did" (Albert T. Clay to Albright, December 14, 1920). See King, *American Archaeology*, 56.

post until his death in 1925.[29] Apparently erratic, alternately charming and tactless, sometimes vindictive, often imperious, Clay seemed a force to be reckoned with. For Albright, a relative newcomer to the circle of Semitists and archaeologists, Clay had to be treated with particular care. Privately, he thought that Clay was "impulsive" and blundering, and that he knew "amazingly little," considering his position, about Assyrian grammar and philology. Although Clay was a good copyist, his translations of Assyriological texts were "sorry things," which made American scholarship a "laughing stock of European Orientalists."[30] Moreover, Albright disparaged Clay's activities in defense of Christianity and biblical literalism for their reckless flamboyancy; and he maligned Clay's public image of righteous defender by citing his private moral failings, or at least what seemed so to an upright and abstemious son of a Methodist missionary.[31]

Albright kept these judgments to himself for the most part. Even before arriving in Jerusalem, he had decided not to offend Clay. Now that they worked together in the Jerusalem school, Albright was determined further to remain diplomatically apart from Clay's vituperative disagreements with others. Since Clay was "too evidently afraid of my superior linguistic and philological attainments," he told his father, "a difficulty with him would probably cost me the chance to get a position later."[32]

29. *The National Cyclopaedia of American Biography*, vol. 22 (New York: James White, 1932), 130–31. See also W. F. Albright's eulogy of Clay, "Professor Albert T. Clay—An Appreciation," *Journal of the Palestine Oriental Society* 5 (1925), 173–77.

30. Albright to his father, William Finley Albright, January 11, 1920.

31. Albright to his mother, Zephine Viola Albright, May 26, 1920. In a remarkable outburst, Albright joined disdain for Clay's poor scholarship with scorn for Clay's fame as a defender of the Bible's truth. Clay's apologetic publications included "Are the Patriarchs Historical?" *Yale Review*, n.s. 2 (1912): 116–29; *Light on the Old Testament from Babel* (Philadelphia: Sunday School Times Co., 1915); "Pushing Back History's Horizon: How the Pick and Shovel Are Revealing Civilizations That Were Ancient When Israel Was Young," *National Geographic Magazine* 29 (1916): 162–216. His sixteen-year campaign to weaken "pan-Babylonism," a tendency to attribute most of the Old Testament materials to borrowings from Mesopotamian predecessors, seemed at bottom a defense of the uniqueness and priority of the Bible. See *Amurru, the Home of the Northern Semites: A Study Showing that the Religion and Culture of the Bible Are Not of Babylonian Origin* (Philadelphia: Sunday School Times Co., 1909; *The Empire of the Amorites* (New Haven: Yale University Press, 1919); *The Origins of Biblical Traditions* (New Haven: Yale University Press, 1923). Albright offered a gentler assessment of Clay several years later. Urging Worrell to lay aside a bitter residue from their disputes during 1919–20, he wrote that Clay was strangely complex—passionate, impulsive, generous, and kindhearted to some extent, but "unbelievably vindictive" toward anyone he thought opposed him. To Albright, however, Clay had always been considerate, "so I can never feel hostile toward him." Nevertheless, Albright added, with Worrell's troubles in mind, "I can see . . . how easily he may be turned into a bitter and ruthless foe." (Albright to William Worrell, January 20, 1924.)

32. Albright to Zephine Viola Albright, April 12, 1919. Albright to William Finley Albright, January 11, 1920.

While developing a close friendship with Worrell (his more moderate views on religion, though not his Unitarianism, probably appealed to Albright), and staying out of the way when tensions rose between Clay and Worrell, Albright apparently tried not to antagonize Clay or offend his evangelical convictions. The situation was such that in May 1920, at a meeting of the newly organized Palestine Oriental Society—Clay had founded the organization and, along with the Dominican Marie-Joseph Lagrange, was presiding over this occasion—Albright felt obliged to announce to the assembled company that his scholarly reconstructions of Solomon's Temple entirely agreed with the biblical account.[33]

While keeping Clay's favor that first year, Albright also traveled throughout the country with John Peters as his companion and archaeological guide.[34] Peters, about forty years Albright's senior, had received his Ph.D. from Yale in 1876 in Sanskrit and comparative philology. He studied Semitics in Germany, and then pursued his career in Bible and archaeology at the Philadelphia Divinity School (1884–91) and the University of Pennsylvania (1885–93). Without forgoing his academic work entirely, he subsequently became an active clergyman in his father's parish, St. Michael's Protestant Episcopal Church in New York City, and served there until 1919. His year at the Jerusalem school had come between parish work and a return to full-time teaching, his last, at the University of the South, in Sewanee, Tennessee.[35]

Albright probably could not have found a more intellectually congenial guide than he found in Peters. Taking for granted the historical reliability of the Bible, Peters investigated the literary sources of the Bible so as to extract authoritative religious doctrine. As reserved in his apologetics as Clay was flamboyant, Peters nevertheless had no doubt that archaeological finds in the main confirmed the biblical versions of history, including the Bible's assumption of its own importance. Two decades earlier, Peters had devoted his presidential address before the Society of Biblical Literature and Exegesis to a spirited defense of the exalted monotheism of Moses, and he used the tools of historical research to inveigh against skeptics who

33. Running and Freedman, *Albright*, 79; King, *American Archaeology*, 56. In Albright's recollection of that meeting (Albright to Wilbur Finley Albright, ca. June or July, 1920), Clay's presence loomed large, not only because of the turmoil in the school that year, but because Clay was prominently associated with the establishment of the Palestine Oriental Society. In this same letter Albright wrote a harsh condemnation of Clay's work, career, and personal behavior.

34. See Running and Freedman, *Albright*, 72–76.

35. See *Dictionary of American Biography*, vol. 14 (New York: Charles Scribner's Sons, 1934), 506–7. I am indebted to M. Patrick Graham of the Pitts Theological Library, Emory University, for other information. A bibliography of Peters's work was published in the *Journal of Biblical Literature* 41 (1922): 246–48.

diminished Moses' stature. Moses was unique, he said, and it was "because he [Moses] was *sui generis*, towering above his race and time, that he was able to found, among a primitive and barbarous people, a religion capable of such wonderful development," which, he could have added, flowered as Christianity.[36] Peters often wrote about recent discoveries in Bible lands, and sometimes, transformed by pious longing, he sounded fervent assurances of a Christian pilgrim:

> It is almost a mile's walk from the house of the Last Supper—down the stair street, past the fountain of Siloam, out of the water gate, turning to the left up the valley of the Kidron, past the priestly tombs, under the great mass of the temple—to the Garden of Gethsemane. They walked between gardens, where just at that time, according to custom, the vines were being trimmed, the cuttings from which had been thrown into the street to wither. You have in the account of Jesus' discourse on the way one of those unconscious eye-witness pictures of the surroundings; how as they walked down that street, they trod on these withering vine branches, and saw the vine stocks from which they had been cut. . . . Who could have invented this; who but an eye-witness have reported it?[37]

Although Albright's early reports of his explorations (they were not excavations) in Palestine were much more restrained, they evoked a similar spirit. It is not difficult to imagine that such a travel companion as Peters would have encouraged, rather than suppressed, Albright's evangelical convictions and his presumption of historicity for the Bible. And besides, Albright had been warned by his teacher, Paul Haupt, to treat Peters with as much diffidence as he extended toward Nies. "Dr. Peters is not a great scholar," Haupt wrote, "but he has a good deal of influence and may help you a great deal. If there should ever be any difference of opinion between Peters and Clay, especially in practical questions, most people will be inclined to side with Peters."[38]

Considering the Jerusalem that was a mix of romantic piety and infant archaeological science, of pilgrimage and nationalist politics, of fund-raising

36. "The Religion of Moses," *Journal of Biblical Literature* 20 (1901): 104.
37. J. P. Peters, *Bible and Spade* (New York: Charles Scribner's Sons, 1922), 237–38. This book grew out of the Bross Lectures at Lake Forest College, a series established in 1879 to call out the "best efforts of the highest talent and the ripest scholarship of the world to illustrate from science . . . and to demonstrate the divine origin and authority of the Christian Scriptures." From the Preface, p. v.
38. Haupt to Albright, July 6, 1920.

and personal animosities, of creating knowledge and building careers, the figure of conversion from skepticism to conviction, delivered from middle age, looks beguilingly simplistic. Had Albright become "liberal" at Johns Hopkins under the tutelage of Paul Haupt, and then con(re)verted to a more traditional stance under the irresistible press of archaeological evidence? He gave that impression to James Nies. But con(re)verted without field experience in archaeology? And with a "chronological key" to the turnabout already in hand before arriving in British Mandate Palestine? What of the press of expectations, social permissions and prohibitions, that helped define the culture of the American School in Jerusalem at that time? Or, taking up Albright's own suggestion to Sam Geiser, had he in a sense reverted to type, that is, reclaimed what had always been his "tendency"?

An Apologist in Baltimore

Albright invoked the last-mentioned perspective two years later in a long letter to Paul Haupt. With florid deference and apology, Albright not only explained his attitudes toward the Bible, but also announced a delicate distancing of student from teacher, disciple from master, son from father. The range of issues that might have been involved seemed to have been reduced to, as he told Haupt, questions of objective history.

"I wish I could follow you more closely in many points," Albright wrote in 1922, "but, for better or worse, I have returned in general to tendencies already fully developed before I came to Johns Hopkins."[39] Explaining himself, Albright mentioned an article soon to be published that was merely a revision of one he had written some thirteen years earlier.[40] While thanking Haupt for setting the highest standards for scientific philology, Albright nevertheless had to admit—his rhetoric suggests the matter was not a matter of choice—that his views on historical matters had remained unchanged during the intervening years.

Albright then got to the delicate point: expressing the distance he now felt from his demanding and imperious *Doktorvater*. "Perhaps after a temporary reaction to conservatism I will see my way clear to follow more closely in your footsteps," he continued, but at present he did not seem able to do that,

39. Albright to Haupt, October 11, 1922.
40. If Albright's reckoning was correct, he would have written the piece in 1909, while an undergraduate at Upper Iowa University.

at least when treating the Bible. Nonetheless, Albright concluded, "I can never forget the unequaled training given in the Old Testament seminary of Johns Hopkins. To it, I owe a very great deal, which I appreciate profoundly, so I hope you will pardon my tendency to go astray in applying the methods learned at your feet."

By admission, Albright's historical views had remained unchanged. Indeed, some elements in Albright's approach to the Bible seem in retrospect to have been fixed long before he went to Baltimore for graduate training with Haupt. Not all of these had to do directly with his upbringing as the son of a Methodist missionary and strict biblical literalist.[41] Albright recalled that during his preteen and teenage years, from about 1897 to 1909, he avidly followed a series of essays on "Archaeology and Biblical Research" published in the *Methodist Review*.[42] Aimed at educated laypeople and clergy, the *Review* offered nontechnical but sophisticated articles on history, theology, social ethics, literature, and public affairs. Many essays engaged the apologetic debates of the day, especially as the claims of science impacted on traditional religious belief.

The unnamed authors who wrote on the Bible and archaeology were traditionalists in their attitudes, but not literalists. Following guidelines set by the editor, William V. Kelley, D.D., they cautiously accepted theories of written sources behind the Bible, firmly believing that the Bible had its origins in both divine inspiration and human response. They were convinced that attention to archaeology would awaken renewed interest in the Bible and help throw light on Old Testament chronology, history, and especially "the origin of religion and the growth of revelation." Moreover, the new finds helped the writers (and indeed the reader who was assumed to be in danger) resist and censure "destructive" literary critics who excessively fragmented the Bible into multiple sources or who doubted the historical truth of what was written.[43]

From the pages of the *Methodist Review*, a young and precocious Albright may have taken on many of these attitudes and nurtured an interest, which became a pressing concern during his college and graduate training, in constructing moderate and scholarly defenses of biblical claims. He probably

41. Running and Freedman, *Albright*, 1–26.

42. Albright to Nolan B. Harmon, April 20, 1947. Albright was trying to identify the authors of the *Methodist Review* essays, possibly as preparation for writing his autobiographical sketch, published in 1948.

43. William V. Kelley (chief editor) explained the reasons and purposes for the new department of Archaeology and Biblical Research in vol. 76 [5th Series, vol. 10] (1894): 135.

read, for example, an essay that legitimated reverent use of the "higher criticism" for traditional Methodists; or one that argued that archaeology confirmed the historical basis behind the tradition of Abraham and the foreign kings in Genesis 14; or a report on the inscriptions of Hammurabi that sought to illustrate the accuracy of details in the Old Testament. Albright would have read, many times over and in diverse ways, such ringing pronouncements as, "The testimony from the monuments is, therefore, all favorable to the conservative view, and the sooner the higher critics will see it the better it will be for biblical criticism."[44]

A bit later, while an undergraduate at Upper Iowa University (he was still reading the *Methodist Review*), Albright published an essay, a prototype of hundreds that were to follow, on discoveries from an Egyptian/Hebrew settlement at Elephantine, an island in the upper Nile River.[45] The article was thoroughly professional by the conventions of the time: scholarly in form, authoritative and objective in tone, firmly wedded to the canons of scientific historiography. Albright aimed to create a fresh synthesis of historical data by joining information from recently discovered inscriptions to biblical texts. He suggested that the Aramaic-speaking peoples at Elephantine were in fact descendants of *biblical* Israelites. In such a case, it is no wonder that he could note near the beginning of the essay that "the value of these discoveries can scarcely be over-estimated, at least by the Old Testament scholar."

Albright presumed without argument that the remains of a temple at Elephantine could "scarcely be dissociated" from the events narrated in Jeremiah 41–44, and moreover, that this biblical account, which tells of Judaeans escaping conditions in Judaea by settling at Tahpanhes in northern Egypt, was to be accepted at face value. Having made these assumptions, he posited that these Judaean exiles subsequently made their way south to Elephantine, where they built the temple and worshiped "Yahweh as

44. Respectively, Camden Cobern, "The Higher Criticism" *Methodist Review*, 5th Series 17 (1901): 92–98; unsigned essays, 5th Series 14 (1898): 138–41; 5th Series 17 (1901): 640–43; 5th Series 14 (1898): 315. Note a book review that extravagantly praised Charles J. Ball's *Light from the East; or, The Witness of the Monuments: An Introduction to the Study of Biblical Archaeology* (London: Eyre & Spottiswoode, 1899) for its conclusion that the various documents from excavations "afford ample proof of the general trustworthiness of Israelitish history, so far as it is the work of writers who lived in and near the times which they describe." (Idem, 5th Series 16 (1900): 141.)

45. William F. Albright, "Recent Discoveries at Elephantine. I," *Upper Iowa Academician* 1 (1911): 18–20. The journal was apparently a publication of the "Genius Club," the "Academia" of Upper Iowa University. In the article, Albright cited the *Methodist Review* as one of his sources of information. An offprint is among the Albright Papers.

conscientiously as in the days of Josiah" (again taking a biblical text, 2 Kings 22–23 just as it is presented). I give an extended quotation so that the web of interlocking assumptions, textual evidence, and rhetorical tropes of confidence—it is a style that Albright would never abandon—may be fully appreciated.

> The Jewish temple of Yahu' was founded before the conquest of Egypt by Cambyses in the year 525, and must have been founded years before this event, as the last days of the Saite dynasty were troubled times for Egypt. This temple foundation, then, can scarcely be dissociated with the events narrated in Jer., Chap. 41–44, which could not have happened more than fifty years before. . . . In the year 568, Nebuchadrezzar, as foretold by Jeremiah, invaded Egypt, and plundered Tahpanhes. It is in the highest degree probable that the Jews [who had come there from Judaea], who seem to have stood in such awe of the Chaldeans and their king, would have retired to upper Egypt [at Elephantine], where there was comparatively little danger of Babylonian invasion. It was at this time and under these circumstances, doubtless, that they built their temple. . . . Elephantine became a second Jerusalem, and the worship of Yahweh was carried on as conscientiously as in the days of Josiah.[46]

For the young Albright, archaeology seemed to serve its highest purpose in amplifying, extending, or illustrating events recorded in the Bible (he would make similar assertions, it will be recalled, about a decade later in Jerusalem).[47] Supporting the effort was an attribution of privileged reliability to the Bible: it was reliable for faith and, in a leap of logic, reliable for what it says of history and ancient religion. In Albright's hands, the inscriptions discovered at Elephantine did not demonstrate this affirmation about the Bible so much as they reinforced the presumption of its reasonableness: the texts could be made to fit plausibly into what the Bible offered and vice versa. The result, of course, was a particular kind of apologia that insinuates rational, or in this case, scientifically historical, grounds for accepting the Bible, if not in all its details, then in its emotional weight as trustworthy book.

Although not obvious in this particular essay on Elephantine, Albright at the time seemed captivated by a particularly idealistic notion of science.

46. Albright, "Recent Discoveries," 18–19.
47. See *BASOR* 6 (May 1992): 9. See also Albright, "Archaeological Discovery in the Holy Land," *Bibliotheca Sacra* 79 (1922): 403.

When adapted to historical researches, he wrote in another undergraduate essay, scientific rationalism or "modernism" offered great possibilities to describe and embrace an enlightened Christian faith in place of reactionary orthodox dogmatism. Enthusiastically he wrote:

> Science illuminates vast stretches of the unknown darkness around us and binds the whole world together in unity of relations. And over the material advance hovers the kindly glow of human brotherhood, warming and uplifting men's hearts as never before. The broad spirit of world-citizenship, transcending the bounds of mere local patriotism, heralds a new day when peace shall reign unendingly among men.

Continuing, Albright glanced briefly at the "phases of this progress, which is inseparably bound with our modernism, both as cause and effect," and then asked rhetorically, "Has our religion alone been unaffected by this great period of transformation and revaluation?" Some resist such changes and cling to a "Christian economy . . . as immutable as the Himalayas." But Albright, essayist now turned ebullient moralist and apologist, exhorted his reader:

> Let the chaff go; men may quarrel over the chaff-like grain, but the essentials are with us. . . . The human God—this is the Desire of Nations—deity incarnate, suffering with us, [came] to save us from our lower selves. What concept nobler, what better able to inspire men with enduring moral zeal! Here lies the heart of our faith—a heart thru [*sic*] which modernism may attune itself with the pulse-beat of suffering humanity. Let the battle rage around this stronghold![48]

Mellowed and tempered by increasing maturity, convictions such as are evident in both these essays probably operated as intellectual governors at Johns Hopkins when the young Albright encountered Paul Haupt. While cooperating with Haupt's investigations of comparative Semitic mythology, and learning the methods of comparative philology that were to be the hallmark of his career, Albright scornfully dismissed Haupt's literary and historical theories whenever they offended his convictions.

48. William F. Albright, "Modernism—the Genius of Our Day," possibly published in the *Upper Iowa Academician*, ca. 1911 or 1912. A signed but undated offprint of the piece is among the Albright Papers; Albright referred to the essay in a letter to Sam Geiser, November 10, 1912.

Fig. 9. Portrait of Paul Haupt at the Johns Hopkins University, ca. 1910. Courtesy of the Ferdinand Hamburger, Jr., Archives of the Johns Hopkins University.

Once, in class, Haupt produced a finely balanced Hebrew text of the Song of Deborah (Judges 5), having excised a host of later editorial additions— this was a typical exercise for a literary "higher critic" following the tradition of Wellhausen. Albright was skeptical and doubted that even the "Lord Yahweh," a term he and other students used for Professor Haupt, could so recover the original writer's thoughts, "especially when a reconstruction of the history of the times is involved."[49] Sometimes Haupt's theories shocked the young Albright's sense of good taste, and this offense, too, was tied up with Albright's reverence toward the Bible as religious and historical truth. "PH out orientals the orientals," he wrote to Sam Geiser. Explaining that Haupt understood Song of Songs 7:2 to refer to the vulva and even "the *hairs* of the vagina!" Albright added, "I doubt very much whether the gifted author would have considered those special features of the Pudenda as such a poetical subject! Prof. H. makes me disgusted sometimes."[50]

49. Albright to his mother, Zephine Albright, November 30, 1913. Similar skepticism was expressed in subsequent letters to Samuel Geiser on December 10, 1913, and January 31, 1914.
50. Albright to Geiser, February 13, 1914.

Fig. 10.   William F. Albright, ca.
1913, while a student at the Johns
Hopkins University. Courtesy of
Leona Running.

Indeed, Albright seemed very much on guard. He took pains to assure
his parents (for their benefit or his own?) that he was not straying from
his Christian convictions, and wrote his mother during his first year that he
hadn't seen fit to "change a single *important* view so far."[51]

Perhaps only massive stubbornness stood in the way; surely it was not self-
confidence, which was hard to summon up before Haupt. "Whatever comes
to pass," Albright wrote to Sam Geiser about a year later, "get that fool
idea about my progress out of your head." Explaining, Albright said he had
"rehearsed" his paper on Balaam before Haupt and another student, Paul
Bloomhardt, and that Haupt had "flayed him alive." He was as "submissive
as a lambkin," but in hindsight Albright justified his torment. All of Haupt's
students endure similar treatment, Albright told Geiser. "Probably I have
the most vulnerable points, so he rakes me the hardest."[52]

A week later, Albright told Geiser to stop bucking him up with talk of
"career," because, after a "grilling of four and a half hours" in a Baltimore

51. Albright to Zephine Albright, January 18, 1914.
52. Albright to Geiser, March 31, 1915.

park, he wasn't sure he could take Haupt's demeaning and humiliating style of instruction. He had been lectured on how much less he knew than Haupt at a similar age, and on the illogical workings of his mind. Further, Haupt demeaned the Germanisms in Albright's speech, including what Haupt called a "shocking inability to pronounce the 'th' in anthropology and philanthropy." Albright added bitterly, "He [Haupt] pronounces *philansropy*, unless he is on his guard."[53]

Albright perhaps thought that the "grilling" had partly to do with his not being clever enough to hide entirely his resistance to some of Haupt's cherished convictions. A year earlier he had sent this same paper on Balaam to a publisher without showing it to Haupt, as he told his mother, "because it interferes with his ubiquitous theories."[54] On another spring afternoon in Roland Park, reading yet another paper before his teacher, Albright seemed relieved that he could confine himself strictly to lexicographical matters. Still smarting under the memory of earlier humiliations, he later explained that Haupt was "in a better humor, as there was no opportunity there for mishandling his delicately [protected] theories." Completely exhausted, Albright said he was finally dismissed on that occasion with much talk about how important "good papers" were to his career. He was then ordered to rewrite them completely in preparation for a meeting of the American Oriental Society. "On the journey to New York we will go over the papers once again," Haupt announced.[55]

Albright's dissertation was even more the site of submission and resistance than these grooming sessions. Writing to Sam Geiser, Albright dreamed of a day beyond this peculiar trial when he could dedicate a book to Geiser and the constancy of their friendship. He quickly veered off, diverted by ambivalent feelings for Haupt. The book would not be his dissertation, he told Geiser. "I should blush to inscribe your name on Professor Haupt's work."[56] Albright reported later that he filed away at least two papers he had written during those Hopkins days because they contained views he had

53. Albright to Geiser, April 6, 1915.

54. Albright to Zephine Albright, March 15, 1914. The paper was published as "The Home of Balaam," *Journal of the American Oriental Society* 35 (1915): 386–90.

55. Albright to Geiser, April 6, 1915. See further, Albright to Geiser, March 19, 1918; April 26, 1916. Despite his suffering, Albright was grateful for his training, for he wrote in the letter of April 6 that "Haupt is really doing a great deal for me, but he does it in such a curious fashion that I can easily understand his failure to attract men to himself."

56. Letter, Albright to Geiser, February 12, 1916. Among Albright's papers are several letters in which Haupt reports extensive revisions he was incorporating into Albright's dissertation as it was prepared for publication.

Fig. 11.   Snapshot of Ruth Norton with Albright's mother, Zephine Viola Albright, ca. 1920. Courtesy of Leona Running.

held for years but chose to keep hidden from Haupt. "I didn't care to court trouble while I was at Prof. Haupt's mercy!" he added.[57]

It may be, however, that during those years of rigorous and humiliating trial, Albright's inclination toward Christian apologia had formed itself into some sort of deferred program. Training with Haupt was the price to be paid.

The day after Christmas 1913, only weeks after beginning his graduate studies, Albright urgently told his mother of a new discovery. Though blind to it earlier, he now saw an intimate connection between biblical criticism (the "higher criticism" of historical and source analysis) and the preachings of social gospel, or the "new Social Movement." The biblical prophets, or as might be said nowadays, a certain hermeneutical construal of these Old Testament figures, was the key to Albright's realization.

On one side Albright pictured conservative Christians who saw the prophets as simply religious preachers. In fact, the young and confident

57. Albright to Paul F. Bloomhardt, December 8, 1922. These essays were finally published two years after Albright arrived in Jerusalem as "The Date and Personality of the Chronicler," *Journal of Biblical Literature* 40 (1921): 104–24 and "The Location of the Garden of Eden," *American Journal of Semitic Languages* 39 (1922): 15–31.

Albright assured his mother, these biblical prophets were "largely social reformers" whose inspired words had been covered by centuries of accretion. The prophets struck at social injustice "with ungloved hands," but "glossators" over the years softened the force of their blows. Warming to his subject, Albright wrote that by condemning higher critics the "orthodox," those antiscientific antihistorical literalists, hold back the progress of Christ's kingdom and allow this pristine truth about the prophets to languish in obscurity. However, the higher critics would reveal "the flaming chariots of Christ's angels, which drive thru the Bible just as Jehu-like today as ever, tho muffled and smoked by accumulated misunderstandings." Such scholars of the Bible—Albright now seemed to be placing himself in the company of both higher critics and biblical prophets—must be reformers inflamed with a prophet's passion and armed with a scientist's cold scrutiny. Suggesting to his mother a reluctance to serve, like the prophets of old, Albright nevertheless imagined himself becoming a prophet-crusader, less to seek social reform than to expose historical truth about the Bible. "Hereafter," he concluded, "instead of considering Biblical Criticism as an unfortunate necessity, tho not without great eventual good, involved by our search for truth, I shall see it as a crusade, which must be forced upon the attention of the world (with caution, and not with too unrestrained zeal)."[58]

Some years after writing these words, Albright finished his graduate training at Johns Hopkins. Having received the tools of historical philology from a teacher who exemplified the Germanic ideals of a *wissenschaftlich* university, Albright at last seemed ready to embark on his reformst crusade and mount the flaming chariots of Christ's angels. He explained to Sam Geiser that he was laying the foundations for a "Christ-myth rationalism," apparently meaning a scientifically explained Protestant Christianity Triumphant. At the time, Albright was preparing a series of new publications in which he would work out "the prehistory of our Christology" as definitively as possible. He would avoid polemics, Albright told Geiser, and not make a direct reference to the Christian scriptures until all the developments leading to them had been set forth. Satisfied that he had at last found "common ground where scientific rationalism and evangelical faith can meet," Albright imagined his mission: against orthodoxy's refusal of scientific criticism, he would mount a quietly fervent, deliberate, and modern defense of Christianity's truth. "During the coming years," he told Geiser, "I shall, if God wills that my eyesight be spared, devote myself quietly to my technical

58. Albright to "Mother," Zephine Viola Albright, December 26, 1913.

researches, incidentally building a structure too strong for the batteries of mistaken apologetics. When it is all over, orthodoxy will rub its eyes and say, wonderingly, 'What was I afraid of? It all seems so reasonable now!' Such are the laws of progress in our society."[59]

I believe it would be a mistake to dismiss these statements as simply overwrought infatuations of youth. In the first place, Albright began his career when many American Protestants were creating forms of theology variously adapted to new forms of social and secular philosophy. Christian biblical critics found themselves caught up in religious controversies, and the decade of the 1920s brought forth strident voices, even the polarizing vocabulary, as "modernists" and "fundamentalists" struggled against one another. Under the circumstances, it would not have been unusual for biblical scholars to shape their work in some measure to meet the needs of Christian apologia, either to resist many of the social and intellectual changes sweeping through America from the 1880s to World War I, or to create bodies of biblical knowledge that would aid the causes of progressive theology.[60]

The second reason that Albright's sense of mission is not to be dismissed too lightly is that after twenty-two years of extraordinarily productive and focused scholarly work, he actually realized these youthful ambitions. He did it soberly, grandly, and with an unrivaled assemblage of the evidence. During World War II, Albright published two substantial books: *From the Stone Age to Christianity* and *Archaeology and the Religion of Israel*.[61] In both, Albright organized massive additions to knowledge about the ancient Near East, many of which were his own discoveries, in the service of that "prehistory" to Christology which he had envisioned at the age of twenty-seven. The books seemed also to have been conceived as successors and correctives to the nontheistic works of James Henry Breasted, especially *The Dawn of Conscience*.[62] Albright opposed what he would later call Breasted's "non-religious teleology," while embracing a Breasted-like ambition to create a

---

59. Albright to Sam Geiser, October 8, 1918.

60. For the wider picture, see Winthrop Hudson, *Religion in America,* 3d ed. (New York: Charles Scribner's Sons, 1981), 265–92; Sidney Ahlstrom, *A Religious History of the American People* (New Haven: Yale University Press, 1972), 763–804; Stow Persons, "Religion and Modernity," in James Smith et al., *The Shaping of American Religion* (Princeton: Princeton University Press, 1961), 369–401; Martin Marty, *Pilgrims in Their Own Land: 500 Years of Religion in America* (Boston: Little, Brown & Co., 1984), 297–317.

61. *From the Stone Age to Christianity: Monotheism and the Historical Process* (Baltimore: Johns Hopkins University Press, 1940); *Archaeology and the Religion of Israel* (Baltimore: Johns Hopkins University Press, 1942).

62. New York: Charles Scribner's Sons, 1933.

unified history of Western religion from its prehistoric beginnings down to early Christian times.[63]

The purpose of *From the Stone Age*, Albright wrote, was to trace "our Christian civilization of the West to its earliest sources." In the 1948 translation into German, Albright added that he hoped to thereby "deliver a small contribution to Christian theology of the future."[64] Two years later Albright wrote that his purpose in publishing *Religion of Israel* was "nothing less than the ultimate reconstruction, as far as possible, of the route which our cultural ancestors traversed in order to reach Judeo-Christian heights of spiritual insight and ethical monotheism." He was mainly concerned, he said, "with the religion of the Old Testament, of which the religion of the New was only the extension and fulfillment."[65]

I read both of these works as, in part, reformist projects which encoded Albright's passion as prophet–historical critic. By transposing traditional theological claims for the uniqueness and truth of biblical revelation into the idiom of objectivist historical narrative, Albright tried to reinstate a condition of belief he thought had been weakened by a broad range of twentieth-century events. For example, in both narratives Albright conceived ancient Israel as an ethnic unity opposed to the Canaanites, who were just as simplistically imagined as culturally and religiously deficient, if not depraved. Given to "orgiastic nature-worship," and "gross mythology," the Canaanites were a people whose "cult of fertility in the form of serpent symbols and sensuous nudity . . . were replaced by Israel, with its pastoral simplicity and purity of life, its lofty monotheism and its severe code of ethics."[66]

Similar contrasts ruled Albright's aesthetic judgments. Assyrian-Babylonian poetry had a "curiously monotonous effect," but Israelite poets took inherited literary conventions, used them "even more effectively" than their

63. Albright greatly admired Breasted, but was troubled by what he called his "meliorism," a strong humanistic faith in the natural order which through human effort becomes better and better. See Albright's memorial tribute, "James Henry Breasted, humanist," in *American Scholar* 5 (1936): 287–99. I have been unable to locate among Albright's papers a document in which, as David Noel Freedman reported to me, Albright had compared his own accomplishments with those of Breasted.

64. *Stone Age*, 32. See *Von der Steinzeit zum Christentum* (Bern: Francke, 1949), 7. Pagination in *Stone Age* refers to the Anchor Books edition (Garden City, N.Y.: Doubleday, 1957), in which the original text was updated mainly with a new introduction and a few additional end notes.

65. *Religion of Israel*, 4. Pagination refers to the Anchor Books edition (Garden City, N.Y.: Doubleday, 1969), the text of which is virtually unchanged from the 1942 edition.

66. *Stone Age,* 281. On the theologically vested stereotyping of the Canaanites, see Delbert Hillers, "Analyzing the Abominable: Our Understanding of Canaanite Religion," *Jewish Quarterly Review* 75 (1985): 253–69.

neighbors had, and preserved "most of the beauties and few of the crudities of older national literature." Even though the emotional heights of biblical poetry could be found in Mesopotamia, Albright wrote, "biblical literature maintains a much higher average level of feeling."[67]

In short, Albright reclaimed his truths about the Bible but valorized them more *against* their environment than *in* it. Or to paraphrase Saint Paul, the Israelites—Albright seems to have conflated the Israel of a canonical theological perspective with historical Israel—the Israelites lived *in* their world, but not *of* it.

Moreover, an ancient structure of Christian (prophetical) historiography ruled *From the Stone Age*. Headings for individual chapters, such as "Praeparatio," or "When Israel Was a Child . . . ," or "In the Fullness of Time . . . ," all invoked Christian and specifically patristic hermeneutics as approved frameworks for properly grasping the import of this scientifically grounded history of ancient religion. The Old Testament was preparation for the New, or in different terms, the Old Testament prophetically configured Christ; or in the idiom of historiography, the religious ideas of the ancient peoples of Near Asia evolved, haltingly, unevenly, "organismically," from primitive beginnings to the highest truths of Christianity.

In addition, in various remarks Albright suggested that this purposive directionality in history was heavily weighted toward Christian self-characterization. Albright detected, for example, a "certain movement in the direction of theological universalism" in Mesopotamian and Egyptian religion, and its flowering in Mosaic monotheism.[68] It is difficult to miss the specifically Christian interest in such a representation. Not only did Albright trace a course of theological universalism through biblical Israel to the early church, but in eventually valorizing constructions of Christian truth, he portrayed a Christianity that had superseded ancient Judaism, whose original universal vision was clouded by lingering ethnic particularism.[69]

Albright believed that the cultural and religious ideas of West Asian peoples demonstrably evolved from primitive beginnings to the highest (and never-to-be-surpassed) truths of Christianity. Accordingly, he built a

67. *Stone Age*, 281; *Religion of Israel*, 14, 21.

68. *Stone Age*, 213.

69. Albright's version of this traditional theological view came to the surface in *Stone Age*, 391–92, where he imagined the strictly monotheistic Pharisees as praiseworthy, but nevertheless just deficient enough to allow for Christian triumph, or in the idiom of Darwinism, something of an evolutionary dead end. The Pharisees were "not at all suited to become the vehicle of a great evangelistic movement," Albright wrote, because they were weighed down with a "mass of secondary regulations and restrictions."

narrative of intellectual and cultural movement toward Christianity out of a theological position: a Jesus-centered, supersessionist reading of all that had gone before—Hebrew, Greek, and their ancient Near Eastern antecedents. Wearing the hats of Christian and historian, Albright finally asserted at the end of *Stone Age* that the "Church Fathers saw truly when they represented these aspects of paganism [the pre-Christian elements of culture] as part of the divine preparation for Christianity."[70] Albright had ridden the flaming chariots of Christ, and, like the prophets of old, called Christians (who were portrayed at the time as engaged in a life-and-death struggle with totalitarianism) back to the pristine roots of their Christology: "We need reawakening of faith in the God of the majestic theophany on Mount Sinai, in the God of Elijah's vision at Horeb, in the God of the Jewish exiles in Babylonia, in the God of the Agony at Gethsemane."[71]

In view of such sweeping claims as these two works presented, and of the indications that Albright had begun to envision some such program of Christian apologetics for himself as early as 1913, surely by 1918 the suggestion made about three decades later that he had been jolted from liberal skepticism to conservative acceptance of the Bible's historical accuracy seems deeply problematic. To me, the captivating simplicity of this figure of speech suggests less than it represents, or represents more than it suggests at first glance. In its ability to mask and disclose at the same time, this verbal gesture draws me to ask after its ideological function. Therein may be found one way to interpret its appeal that others, Albrightean sons and grandsons or not, found irresistible.

A Mythic Paradigm

Albright was a positivist historian and Christian, and was convinced that the data of history had to be, and could be, liberated from the clutches of subjectivity. Thus, when asked to write the sketch in which this figure of conversion appeared, he devoted two pages to wrestling with his discomfort at writing autobiography. A troubling form of historical writing, autobiography deals with personal idiosyncrasy beyond statistical control, he wrote, and therefore is very difficult to master. Moreover, autobiography is suspect, because a

70. *Stone Age*, 399.
71. *Stone Age*, 403.

writer lacks distance and perspective, and easily succumbs to temptations to "readjust and color" facts to one's own advantage.

Apparently ambivalent beyond simple or feigned modesty, Albright nevertheless took up the task. He submitted to his usual historicist principles, assuming that his more-accustomed mode of historical inquiry, the familiar grounding of a trained and rational historian, equipped him to escape the dangers he had conjured up. He then abruptly adopted third-person language. "In the following concise spiritual autobiography," he wrote, "the subject will attempt to appraise his own development, in the light of the more pertinent facts of his education," followed by a discussion of themes where "the subject's" views had been "most clearly influenced by the external facts of his education and experience."[72]

By writing himself out of his own autobiography in this fashion, Albright seemed to imply that he had overcome the obstacles he had mentioned. The language of distance and control, which kept errant subjectivity at bay, seemed calculated to assure a reader, and perhaps Albright himself, that "subjective judgments on his own development as far as possible" had been avoided.[73] Thus when it entered the narrative a few pages later, that seductive figure of passage from skepticism to conviction would seem inoculated against anything that might have rendered it problematic.

From another perspective, however, I would suggest that Albright's rhetoric of effacement replaced the constructing self, the scholar who creates meaning, with a reified artifact of Self. Albright obscured the willing, desiring, choosing, and speaking (writing) subject-person, the Albright who emerges out of language and maps reality through language, that is, who creates understandable "world" linguistically.[74] Under the paradigmatic imperatives of objectivist historical inquiry, Albright effaced this constructor of narrative and metaphor, and put in its place a commanding Self, the Master Knower.

When Albright remembered his passing from skepticism to conviction, I would suggest, he selectively re-*member*ed that experience in ways that reduced and simplified its complex psychological, linguistic, and social dynamics. But he did something else, more implicit, perhaps more powerful: he located a reified Master Knower Self within an implied charter narrative

---

72. Finkelstein, *American Spiritual Autobiographies*, 157.

73. Curiously, when Albright reprinted this essay in 1964, he vacillated between first- and third-person style, as though his ambivalence about autobiography had been preserved. See *History, Archaeology, and Christian Humanism* (New York: McGraw Hill Book Co., 1964), 301–7, 311, 312.

74. See Chapter 1, above.

of modernist criticism, in a moment of scientific discovery. The Self could do
no other than abandon ignorance for knowledge.

Following a dominant strain within the Enlightenment philosophical tradition, Albright assumed the knowing Self to be an autonomous, stable,
rational "subject" who was capable of speaking truth about a stable and
knowable "object" (that which is not-self) in language that corresponded,
if refined through competent reason, directly to "reality out there." Within
this framework, the aim of scientific rationality was to master the physical
and social environment (for Albright, master even the "object" of autobiographical attention). Thus, when Albright took up the autobiographical
form, he projected that Master Knower Self onto a fictive landscape of
positivistic modernism or scientific rationality. In the figure of conversion,
he summoned up a paradigmatic first awakening of autonomous Master Self
(which stands outside the material and social production of knowledge and
is free to define and understand). Perhaps more covertly, he also blended
Master Self with that Albright-specific Crusader Self, who joins battle to
defeat ignorant opponents of scientifically rationalized religious truth (the
enemy Wellhausen, whose theories on ancient Israel's religious history were
"incredible," and besides, "contradicted by all the facts of Egyptology and
Assyriology").[75] The figure of passage posited the Self's first embrace of
values and convictions that helped define "how things really are" in the
world of science and (true) Christianity, a world of intellectual endeavor in
which the Bible is scientifically, religiously, and rightly understood.

And how *are* things naturally, truly, eternally, according to the implied
modernist myth of scientific knowledge? What are some of those beliefs
and values, the "givens" that, once taken on as natural truths, resided in the
foundational structure of Albright's work?

First, recall Albright's commitment to paradigms of empirical "science"
and historical knowledge. Albright was convinced that viewing reality "out
there" through historical and empirical consciousness offered the only reliable access to truth, including much, but not all, of what people identify as
religious truth. In 1958, Albright confessed in print what had always been
implicit in his work: a lifelong opposition to all systems of thought that were
"based on arbitrary postulates and [on] denying or disregarding the historical
experience of mankind." He dismissed on one side speculative philosophies
that were removed from empirical verification and, on the other side, he
opposed "rigorously pragmatic and instrumental" philosophical systems,

75. Finkelstein, *American Spiritual Autobiographies,* 165.

since they "reject anything that cannot be determined experimentally or mathematically." Albright placed himself in the middle: a champion of empiricism, shaped by rational philosophical thought, but suspicious of what he called "exaggerated philosophical emphases" that would deny the need for religion or the nonmaterial realities of which it speaks.[76] Albright was so much a child of the Enlightenment and nineteenth-century historicism in this regard that he dismissed what he called the "escapist" (nonhistoricized) religions of Asia as "out of touch with reality." He thought that because they lacked historical awareness, Asian civilizations were ill-equipped to adapt to a modern technological world.[77]

Second, there was Albright's belief in the "facts" of ancient history— discoverable by scientific modes of investigation. The past may be known objectively, but through sophisticated use of analogy, if one pays attention to the sure and unfailing evidence that convicts. Albright devoted his most sustained effort to these matters in *Stone Age*, and offered his readers a view of how systematic application of "modern archaeological and philological methods" had decisively altered the philosophy and epistemology of history, that is, the very notions of "history" and how one can know it. Like many other historians of the day, he combined an evolutionary developmental narrative with a scientific model: observation, induction, and theorizing— obtaining "factual data" and determining "whether they may be considered certain, probable, possible, improbable, or impossible."[78]

Third, recall that Albright treated the Bible as theologically and culturally privileged text, and the Bible's creators as the privileged voices from the ancient world. It was a Bible presumed to be the source of revelatory

76. William F. Albright, "Return to Biblical Theology," *Christian Century*, November 19, 1958, reprinted in *History, Archaeology, and Christian Humanism*, 287–300. See especially, 289–90. See also "The Impact of Archaeology on Biblical Research—1966," David Noel Freedman and Jonas Greenfield, eds., *New Directions in Biblical Archaeology* (Garden City, N.Y.: Doubleday, 1971), 6.

77. Albright harshly criticized Toynbee *(An Historian's Approach to Religion* [New York: Oxford University Press, 1956]) for his low opinion of biblical religion and his admiration of Hinduism, which, to Albright, was "polytheism and nature-worship, with a philosophical facet which remains far more out of touch with reality (since the phenomenal world is simply *maya* 'illusion') than the Greek philosophical systems." Western Christian civilization, heir to both Hebraic and Greek philosophies, and imbued with historical awareness, is "sweeping the world" and is better adapted to a new age of technology than the "illusionist and escapist faiths of the East." Albright's review was first published in the *Baltimore Evening Sun* (September 11, 1956), and was reprinted in *History, Archaeology, and Christian Humanism*, 250–55.

78. *Stone Age*, 25–26. See also Albright's *Archaeology, Historical Analogy and Early Biblical Tradition* (Baton Rouge: Louisiana University Press, 1966).

truth, and unlike secular documents from the ancient world, presumed to be historically reliable as well. Albright configured the Bible as radically different from, but related to and illuminated by, those lesser cultures all about, such as the Canaanites with their "gross mythology" and poetry of less fine feeling. Thus, archaeology and the broad range of "Oriental" studies, a term that now suggests a European gaze upon western Asia, achieved their highest purposes in "illustration, elucidation, and, if need be, confirmation of this masterpiece of world literature."[79] Yet, Albright's object of scientific inquiry was constructed not out of literary discourse, that is, as text-writing-literature (on his ideological map, it will be recalled, William Irwin and the University of Chicago were dismissed for following this "error"). It was rather Bible-illuminated-and-glossed (and reaffirmed in the main as historically accurate) against a background made visible by archaeological/historical research.

Fourth, there was the biblical archaeology crusade authorized in the narrative of the dawning new era. Study of ancient civilizations offered the necessary means to overcome the sterile impasse of a waning age of literary and textual study of the Bible, and also, the theological poverty of a liberal and skeptical generation of biblical scholars. It was to Albright and his sons that initiative for the crusade fell. They were equipped to reclaim the Bible from the arid and subjective clutches of literary theorists and, moreover, to rescue the Bible from literalists on one side and skeptics on the other. The Albrighteans aimed to explain the Bible in its historical context, and at the same time confirm this illuminated and glossed object as historically reliable and theologically relevant to the modern day. Thus they served up background commentary that more by implication than examination assured a Bible user that the book was consistent with sensibilities of modern people.

Fifth, Albright seemed to view himself as enacting a narrative of scientific progress. A scientifically oriented biblical scholar is driven to discover the new, to suppress one's own subjectivity in the act of accumulating fact upon fact, building structures of knowledge that are presumed to confirm, not so much all the details, but the emotional weight, of a trustworthy Bible. Albright valued change as evolutionary "progress" and, with an overarching theistic faith in divine guidance ("there *is* Intelligence and a Will, expressed

---

79. William F. Albright, "Archaeological Discovery in the Holy Land," *Bibliotheca Sacra* 79 (1922): 403. See also, "Archaeology Confronts Biblical Criticism," *American Scholar* 7 (1938): 176–88; "The Archaeological Background of the Hebrew Prophets," *Journal of Bible and Religion* 8 (1940): 131–36.

in both History and Nature," he wrote),[80] he put progressive betterment
at the base of his "organismic" philosophy of history. In his view, human
cultures were likened to patterned behavior of unified biological organisms;
cultures evolved (and are evolving) from lower to higher, by fits and starts
of advancement and regression, just as living organisms do.[81] A scientific
approach provides knowledge of these matters, and so is implicated in
the energies that led to high valuation of the newly discovered, the up-
to-date, the ever revisable. Progress is never sufficient to end the quest
for increased understanding, for the idealized paradigms of science specify
iterative discovery and willingness to adapt theory to data, while naturally
leaving quite undisturbed the foundational structures of modernist inquiry.[82]

Albright clearly thought of himself as a scientist.[83] This self-image does
not seem to have been simply a matter of youthful infatuation, as one might
have gathered from his essay on "modernism." He was in fact well read in the
various scientific disciplines of his day, especially mathematics, physics, and
biology. As a high school principal, fresh out of college, he enthusiastically
taught mathematics and science, and he assiduously cultivated those few
pupils who showed aptitude in science.[84] He extolled theories of the great
scientific thinker Poincaré[85] and advised Sam Geiser, then a young teacher
of biology, "Don't try to master science, but let science master you—as
she always has."[86] In his middle years, Albright dreamed of establishing
an academy of humanistic science and scientific humanism,[87] and to some
extent his active participation in the affairs of the American Philosophical
Society and the History of Ideas Club at Johns Hopkins helped him realize

80. *Stone Age*, 126.

81. *Stone Age*, 82–126.

82. Albright frequently referred to his willingness to change his mind on various philological
or historical details; his students spoke of this feature of their teacher's work and defended it
as a mark of his scientific temperament. See, for example, Frank Moore Cross, Jr., "William
Foxwell Albright: Orientalist," *BASOR* 200 (1970): 7–11; Yigael Yadin, "William Foxwell
Albright," *Eretz-Israel* 9 (1969): ix–xii. These and other tributes were reprinted in David
Noel Freedman, ed., *The Published Works of William Foxwell Albright: A Comprehensive
Bibliography* (Cambridge, Mass.: American Schools of Oriental Research, 1975). For a study
of Albright's celebrated changes of mind, see Stanley E. Hardwick, *Change and Constancy in
William Foxwell Albright's Treatment of Early Old Testament History and Religion, 1918–1958*
(Ph.D. diss., New York University; Ann Arbor: University Microfilms, 1965).

83. See Running and Freedman, *Albright*, 287.

84. Albright to his father, William Finley Albright, January 12, 1913.

85. Albright to father, December 15, 1912.

86. Albright to Geiser, October 26, 1913.

87. Albright to Geiser, October 31, 1929.

the dream. In old age he admitted, perhaps only half jokingly, to being a "frustrated scientist at heart."[88]

I do not view Albright's sense of self-as-scientist, with its commanding image of autonomous Self as Master Knower, as simply a matter of individual preference or expression of some inner essence of his "true self." Adopting a postmodern viewpoint, as indicated in Chapter 1, I understand self as a linguistic construct built out of, and in relation to, a complex and interactive social world. From this perspective Albright's self-image and his work as "Orientalist" were both embedded in the discourse of scientific rationality. The notion of autonomous knowing Self grew out of the post-Enlightenment culture of reason, whose symbolic underpinnings were set forth and nurtured prominently within a culture of scientific practice.

When Albright came of age, this ethos of science took a particularly heroic form. Books, popular magazines, and even such sedate media as the Proceedings of the National Academy of Sciences honored living scientists (frequently dead ones too) by turning them into romantic figures. Such scientific heroes were dedicated to selflessness, truth, and an austere life-style which, in its elevating purity, could, like great religious leaders, inspire and motivate people less given to sacrificial greatness.[89] Scientists were knights whose features remained remarkably static in popular magazines. Brilliant, hardworking, and modest, they mixed qualities of wizard, creator/destroyer, and hero.[90] Scientists, imaged in the patterns and colors of heroic myth, struggled to set the mind free of superstition and dogma; emboldened by a sense of righteousness, they marched forth to lift humanity from its primitive imperfections and set it on its way to maturity. For the theist-scientist-hero (and there were many such people eulogized in the Proceedings of the National Academy), such efforts to release humanity from its imprisonment did the bidding of a God who nudged evolution toward increasing perfection and, for human beings, more perfect apprehension of divinity.[91]

88. Albright, "Impact of Archaeology," 6.

89. See Charles Rosenberg, *No Other Gods: On Science and American Social Thought* (Baltimore: Johns Hopkins University Press, 1961), 3.

90. On this persistent mythification of science, see especially: Marcel LaFollette, *Making Science Our Own: Public Images of Science, 1910–1955* (Chicago: University of Chicago Press, 1990); John Burnham, *How Superstition Won and Science Lost: Popularizing Science and Health in the United States* (New Brunswick: Rutgers University Press, 1987).

91. See Harold Faulkner, *Quest for Social Justice* (New York: Macmillan, 1931), chaps. 6–10, for the impact of science and technology on American life. For the scientist/theist, see, for example, *A Memoir of Samuel George Morton, M.D.* (Philadelphia: National Academy of Sciences, 1851); "Memoir of Ogden Nicholas Rood" (Washington, D.C.: National Academy of

If his essay "Modernism" is any indication, the young Albright clearly had appropriated a good measure of the romance associated with science and scientists when he embarked on graduate training. He also chose a school that carried in its sense of institutional purpose a historic commitment to many of these same ideas and sentiments. Since its founding in 1876, the Johns Hopkins University had been guided by the ideals of the German "scientific" research university. Its first president, Daniel Coit Gilman, promulgated a dictum that, because of its defining importance, every subsequent president had somehow to reenact: "Wherever there is knowledge, there is science; and wherever there is a science there should be a hearty maintenance of it by all educated men."[92] According to Albright's colleague John Walton, a professor of education, this ruling ideology of science was so strong at Johns Hopkins that the humanities suffered, and even great humanists on its faculty were underappreciated.[93]

In 1948, when Albright construed his beginnings in Jerusalem and left us with a mythic artifact of Self as Master Knower and crusader-prophet-reformer-apologist, I believe that he did not simply draw on his personal history and convictions. He also drew deeply on the formative myths and value-laden scientific ethos of the Johns Hopkins University, and the more generalized mythic dimensions of early twentieth-century scientific practice.

One way to see Albright fully within this complex ideational and social reality is to suggest that he implicitly put himself—I mean the reified Self—onto a mythic landscape of science and scientists, and at the same time defined this moment of awakening within an authorizing narrative of Albrightean-styled biblical archaeology, with its explicit but often effaced interest in religious apologetics. This moment of conversion also encapsulated a powerful join of two paradigmatic images, both of which were at the heart of modernist thought: science as empirical discovery, and self as autonomous knower. Thus, the mythologized Albright awakened to knowledge on the basis of *empirical* experience and, moreover, linked the persuasive power of this motif to the commonsense authority of *personal* experience enshrined in scientifically controlled and restrained autobiographical narrative.

Sciences, 1905), esp. p. 450. Of the many books that helped members of the general public to sustain the image of scientist as mythic hero, see Charles Gibson, *Heroes of the Scientific World: An Account of the Lives, Sacrifices, Successes, and Failures of Some of the Greatest Scientists in the World's History* (London: Seeley, Service & Co., 1913).

92. From his 1897 address, quoted by John C. French, *A History of the University Founded by Johns Hopkins* (Baltimore: Johns Hopkins University Press, 1946), 440.

93. Leona Running, transcript of interview of John Walton (July 5, 1972). By courtesy of Leona Running.

Fig. 12.   William F. Albright as scientist examining artifact,
ca. 1955. Courtesy of the Ferdinand Hamburger, Jr., Archives
of the Johns Hopkins University.

With such structures of thought, I suggest, Albright supported his view of
biblical archaeology as scientific discipline, and through these same images
he configured its history as a teleological narrative of urgent, fast-paced
discovery with revolutionary consequences. In one influential survey of the
field, he featured Master Knowers, "geniuses," each of whom "advanced the
sum of knowledge" in the field, made archaeology increasingly "scientific,"
and helped others progress steadily toward a "remote goal of a complete

archaeological history of Palestine." Joined to this primary narrative was a secondary one that told how a historically trustworthy Bible was being recovered thanks to the "innumerable finds," which no true empiricist, least of all Albright, could deny. Projecting the reified Self as Knower into the narrative, and suppressing dissent with the presumed authority of irreducible experience, Albright concluded:

> The results of these excavations have naturally made an ineffaceable impression on his [Albright's] mind, an impression confirmed by innumerable finds of other archaeologists. Biblical historical data are accurate to an extent far surpassing the ideas of any modern critical students, who have occasionally tended to err on the side of hypercriticism.[94]

Insofar as Albright represented the field for many Americans as it developed from about 1920 well into the post–World War II era,[95] his "story" became an important aspect of how American, and to some extent, Israeli biblical archaeologists, saw themselves and their academic field. In short, Albright's fictive moment of conversion became a mythic paradigm for the field. It was, or better it articulated, an authorizing motif which encoded for a whole generation of Albrighteans some of those values, foundational assumptions, and political aims which were specific to Albright's practice of biblical archaeology.

Many subsequent biblical archaeologists, whether practicing or armchair, reenacted in various ways this paradigm. For example, Ernest Wright's *Biblical Archaeology* inscribed, at least in part, the master narrative of empiricism and carried much farther the theological motivations at the base of his

94. W. F. Albright, *The Archaeology of Palestine* (Baltimore and London: Penguin, 1949), 229. See also chap. 2, "The Discovery of Ancient Palestine," 23–48. Much the same perspective, though with much more emphasis on religious apologetics, may be found in *The Archaeology of Palestine and the Bible* (New York: Fleming H. Revell Co., 1932).

95. P. R. S. Moorey (*A Century of Biblical Archaeology* [Cambridge: Lutterworth, 1991]), puts Albright and his students at the center of a "golden age" of biblical archaeology, 1925–48 (pp. 54–86), and sees the subsequent changes in relation to Albright: the "passing of the old order," a growing "crisis of confidence," and finally, the "eclipse" of Albright's paradigm under the press of growing secularization of the field and a new generation of archaeologists trained more broadly in social scientific models of historical research. See also George E. Mendenhall, "Biblical Interpretation and the Albright School," in Leo Perdue et al., eds., *Archaeology and Biblical Interpretation: Essays in Memory of Dr. Glenn Rose* (Atlanta: John Knox Press, 1987), 3–13; Gus W. Van Beek, ed., *The Scholarship of William Foxwell Albright: An Appraisal*, Harvard Semitic Studies 33 (Atlanta: Scholars Press, 1989).

teacher's work. Wright constructed the history of biblical archaeology as a narrative of developing "science": iterative discovery, increasing precision of method and results, supplantation of old with the new, amassing reliable "data." All was shaped by a teleology of illumination, but explicitly understood as restoring a freshly explained Bible to its place of religious authority. Joining Enlightenment rationalism to religious devotion, the Master Knower moved from ignorance to knowledge. No longer was the Bible a thing of obscurity, a vestigial deposit which "pre-history" left behind like "a monstrous fossil." Nor was the knower any longer without tools of knowing. Now, a biblical archaeologist could read the fossil, and show it to be "testimony to the especial work of God in man's first great age, by which its meaning and his Lordship over all ages is affirmed." Through innumerable points made plain by archaeology, Wright (and he implies any competent biblical archaeologist would agree) reestablished the Bible to its privileged place in modern society.

> We can now see that though the Bible arose in that ancient world, it was not entirely of it; though its history and its people resemble those of the surrounding nations, yet it radiates an atmosphere, a spirit, a faith, far more profound and radically different than any other ancient literature. The progress of archaeology, of textual, literary, and historical criticism has never obscured the fact that the biblical writers were the religious and literary giants of ancient times, though they themselves would never have said so.[96]

In such ways, I would suggest, Albright and his "sons" enacted the mythic paradigm of scientific discovery and religious assurance, and thereby molded, for a time, a culture of generational and ideological solidarity. Herein may be found a reason that the story of Albright's figure of conversion, from skepticism to conviction, proved so repeatable. It was part of the authorizing narrative to be told again and again in a community of like-minded

---

96. G. E. Wright, *Biblical Archaeology* (Philadelphia: Westminster Press, 1962 [1st ed. 1957]), 27. See Wright's earlier claims to the Bible's theological triumphalism in *The Challenge of Israel's Faith* (Chicago: University of Chicago Press, 1944), 14. Cf. Wright, "Biblical Archaeology Today"; David Noel Freedman and Jonas Greenfield, *New Directions in Biblical Archaeology* (Garden City, N.Y.: Doubleday, 1971), 167–86. The "fossil" metaphor, as indeed the narrative framework for the story of biblical archaeology, apparently derived from Albright. See "Recent Discoveries in Bible Lands," Suppl. to Young's *Analytical Concordance to the Bible* (New York: Funk & Wagnalls, 1936), 1–2.

individuals. Whether the mechanism was autobiographical trope, or manuals of biblical archaeology, or activities of the Biblical Colloquium, or the graduate program at Harvard, or planning for a theological dictionary, Albright was *present* and *presented* in the language of scholarship; he was followed, amplified, and revered.

This effort to realize the father was remarkable for its collective ambition and will to dominate American biblical scholarship, especially, but not solely, in producing a wholly new set of standard reference works in the field. The list reads like an inventory of generic monuments to biblical knowledge, some finished and others, even in abandonment, intimating glories of what might have been. Recall John Bright's history of ancient Israel, which joined confidence in the Bible with archaeological data, confidently read (and which was meant to displace its German rival); Ernest Wright's essays on Old Testament theology, which sought the truths of God in the tales of biblical events, made sure by artifact and heart (and which was thought to supplant what Wright and Albright took to be the tepid Bible of tired theological liberalism); the theo(philo)logical dictionary, conceived to wrest both ancient meaning and timeless nurture from concepts (and so displace the merely and inadequately linguistic and historical lexica of biblical languages); Wright's hopes for a comprehensive set of biblical commentaries, only indirectly realized in the *Anchor Bible*, that would blend the popular "salvation-history" notions about biblical thought with Albrightean insistence on profiling a privileged Bible against its pagan environment; the instantiation of an Albrightean way in graduate courses at Harvard and generations of students trained by Cross, Wright, and, in a few years, by some of their own students who joined the Harvard faculty.

Of course, the sons and grandsons would develop nuanced differences from the father. Frank Cross, for example, took up a history of religions program of study, eschewing Albright's overlay of Christian apologetics while retaining his teacher's application of typology to ancient scripts and his interest in maintaining historical value of the Bible.[97] Yet, allowing for

---

97. A recent student remarked that Professor Cross felt "if you were a true scientist, you don't engage in these sorts of [apologetic] issues." Transcript of interviews, 1994. See Frank Moore Cross, Jr., *Canaanite Myth and Hebrew Epic: Essays in the History of the Religion of Israel* (Cambridge, Mass.: Harvard University Press, 1973). This book finely illustrates Cross's break with Albright's theological program, and at the same time shows his indebtedness, as Cross freely acknowledged, to elements of Albright's pioneering approach to ancient texts. See also Cross's appraisal of Albright's work as a typologist, which indirectly testifies to the formative power of this method on Cross's own work, in Gus W. Van Beek, ed., *The Scholarship of William*

differences, many of Albright's other ideological commitments, his authorizing narratives, became, at least for some, the natural truths of biblical and archaeological study, of a believed Bible illuminated, yet distinguished from, its background in the ancient world.

Foxwell Albright: An Appraisal, Harvard Semitic Monographs 33 (Cambridge, Mass.: Harvard University Press, 1989), 17–31.

5   A Retrospective

"I have one mischievous question," John Collins wrote to me. "Does the theory make any difference in how we proceed in practice?"[1]

In a sense the question arose out of our time of disruptive breaks in consensus as to what biblical scholars are supposed to do: Are they modernists or postmodernists? And, as one or the other, or as both, are they historians? literary critics? liberationist cultural critics? theologians? historians of religion? critics of the culture of criticism? Answers must await their own time. Postmodern paths are not well marked or developed. Some say the road less traveled has already lost its allure. With respect to the essays in this book, readers are perhaps better able than I to judge how far along I have gotten. Yet, question begets question, and although it was posed in the last of a series of letters to me—perhaps Collins and I were exhausted by the exchange—the query continues to invite reflection, or perhaps, another letter. What follows could be its substance.

The inclusive "we" in your question, John—I mean in the phrase "make any difference in how we proceed"—in a way, the "we" inhibits my answer. If the pronoun refers to our scholarly community, it seems to enfold my challenge of difference into an embrace of sameness, as though critically trained scholars agree on substance and differ only on inconsequential

1. See Chapter 1.

details. Despite theoretical considerations, the "we" might presume that there is still some kind of unified basis on which *we* carry on. In short, the shift in theoretical perspective I have adopted seems not to have been allowed its impact on the fundamentals. Scholars should be able to play the game as before, you imply, sharing the foundational assumptions of historical, scientific rationalism, but with altered tone and perhaps lessened confidence.

Yet, I have suggested a fundamentally altered foundation on which to build, and the edifice is not entirely square with your consensual "we." The differences have to do not only with how I *think* about knowledge-making, that is, trying not to assume those premises at home in essentialist philosophy and the scientific rationalism of the European enlightenment, but how I go about *constructing* knowledge starting from different epistemological premises.

Albright, and indeed virtually all biblical scholars of midcentury America, can fairly represent what, in a construction of dissent, has been called modernism, by which I mean a worldview rooted in the exalted rationalism of the Enlightenment and expressed above all with images and practices of mastery. Master Knowers, fully self-aware and dominant over nature, set forth to understand, control, and manipulate a world of objects.[2] When these Enlightenment values were allied with a tradition of metaphysical idealism, biblical scholars shaped their modernist practice in the light of two fundamental convictions. First, by disciplined use of scientific reasoning one could in principle fully understand meanings of biblical words, concepts, or historical events in all their time-bound particularities as well as—here metaphysics came into play—in their *a*historical essence. Second, if deployed in a similar spirit, metaphysics could sort out and codify convictions that some human ideas and behavior directly mirrored mandates and patterns of timeless reality. For biblical theologians such as Ernest Wright, this meant that despite disclaimers and qualifications, precise descriptions of biblical concepts pointed to essential verities of God visible in and through, but different from, the historical circumstances of biblical writers and even postbiblical scholar-theologians themselves.

Of course, it is from a "postmodern" standpoint that I have associated this bundle of commitments with "modernism." My narratives about the Albrighteans have drawn upon certain aspects of this wide-ranging, variegated, dialectical, and ironic critique of Enlightenment rationality that runs

---

2. See Andreas Huyssen, *After the Great Divide: Modernism, Mass Culture, Postmodernism* (Bloomington: Indiana University Press, 1986).

through popular culture as well as critical discourses on the arts, linguistics, history, law, literature, politics, and the social sciences.[3] Something clearly has happened to evoke such broad dissent from an intellectual tradition that had hitherto seemed self-evident to largely white, educated, and socially privileged bearers of classical Eurocentric culture.

I do not believe that postmodernism is simply *anti*modern, or merely one generation's rhetorical displacement of its predecessors. The word denotes a jumble of phenomena, or rather altered conditions of knowing that I, and others, have come to recognize all around ourselves. Complicated by peculiar conceptual and social instabilities, the concept itself evokes what it wishes to surpass. It is complicitous with the very tradition it undercuts. Postmodern critique resists, for example, the analytical power of binary opposites, such as subject/object, universal/particular, while claiming space for dissenting thought within, and in relation to, many a binary construct, including the "modern" embedded within postmodern. "Modernism and postmodernism are not separated by an Iron Curtain or a Chinese Wall," one observer recently wrote, "for history is a palimpsest, and culture is permeable to time past, time present, and time future."[4] I stand implicated in such ambiguities, trying to honor both filiation and revolt. I live out of modernist pathways of study that have been very productive for biblical scholarship, and yet I am discovering added layers of scholarly endeavor that can be built on altered, but not entirely distinct, epistemological assumptions.

Undoubtedly my results are less successful and my practices less thoroughly revamped than they might be. This matter, too, shall have its time, and will need to be evaluated in the light of my framing discourse. Anyway, I do not imagine a clear break between modernist and postmodernist sensibilities. Nor do I suppose the latter can live without in some sense drawing nurture from the former.

What difference *has* the theory made?

First, consider the form of the book. I have resisted closure (you will note that this chapter offers no final summary of conclusions) for the same reason that I have avoided a master narrative of the Albrighteans. I have tried not to take up the posture of Master Knower, although not without the temptation of replacing one hegemony, a biographer's appreciation of Albright, for example, with another, my postmodern narratives about

3. See Chapter 1, note 3.
4. Ihab Hassan, *The Postmodern Turn: Essays in Postmodern Theory and Culture* (Columbus: Ohio State University Press, 1987), 88.

Albrightean practices. I suspect mastery and control because it often can obscure, even seek to destroy, difference and dissent. What is more, the aspiration toward mastery of knowledge, that drive to grasp the *real* truth, the single truth about a matter, implies the paradigm of modernist scientific rationalism which I have put aside. I have not thought it useful in this study to imagine myself as a knower who controls external object-world. I have constructed narratives about events, certainly with an eye toward persuading others that my frameshots plausibly open up realities as perceived and acted upon by Albright and his students. I have constructed not so much objective "events" as perspectivities of event-making. At least, that is what I wanted to suggest could be done.

Rather than offer a grand history of Albright, therefore, I have written essays about people interacting with one another and creating their events and situations. I present stories of contest along the fault lines of other scholars' grander narratives of advancement and progress. Some may think the episodes not worth the trouble—a private organization of fewer than a dozen scholars; a dictionary that was never published; a metaphor used by Albright when he became, at least as rhetorical posture, a reluctant autobiographer. However, these occasions provided me with opportunities to explore a range of postmodern concerns: the exercise of power to create Albrightean-framed knowledge and sustain the social relations that maintained its commanding influence (the Biblical Colloquium); conceptual, ideological, and social tensions that weakened confidence in claims to objectivity and normativeness, met by resistance (the theological dictionary); fragments of narratives that bear images and symbols of social identity, the plotted paradigms of *archē* and *telos* that encoded values and programmatic authority for the "Baltimore school" (the myth of supplantation; the Albrightean Self projected into authorizing narratives of science).

I did not look for knowledge scrubbed clean and combed, although I have worked to achieve readable prose. And I have thought striving for some coherence and thematic continuity an act of charity to my readers. Yet, I wanted to preserve ambiguity in "what happened," or rather, to act on my assumption that what happened is inseparably bound to interrelated perspectives on what happened. Historiography, therefore, creates a narrative of competing memories, and is as caught in a web of perspectivity as the actors themselves. I have tried, therefore, to convey dissonant viewpoints and competing interests, not purchase a claim to be final arbiter on how Albright and his students practiced biblical criticism. I am misunderstood, and my topic is misconstrued, John, if you take *my* perspective to be somehow more valuable, more correct, than viewpoints expressed by the characters in my narratives, or by other observers of Albright and his students, for that matter. I am implicated, as they seemed to be, in competing struggles to make sense of what is given, although, as I mentioned earlier, the codes and rhetorical habits of modernist historical writing subvert postmodernist ideology and desire.

Second, consider that the topics of my essays spring from certain questions generated by postmodern theory. Because I assume that knowledge is hermeneutical construct, a matter of relation and perspective to what is given rather than discovery and possession of, or submission to, the "thing-itself," I have created perspectival narratives about perspectivity in Albrightean knowledge-making. I have offered frame-shots of ideological and political interests—you will recall the pedestal of privilege given Albright's archaeologically based backgrounds approach to the Bible, and the way Ernest Wright and John Bright joined this privilege to normative Christian theology; or Albright's drive to support a presumption of the Bible's historical trustworthiness; and his lifelong interest in asserting supersessionally Christian claims to final religious truth. The theory suggests that I look for such things, although I do not expect to see them everywhere.

My theoretical parameters, like a frame, help to set these themes in high relief against the jumbled complexity of memory. I bring them into focus by making visible an Albright present and presented in a culture of generational and ideological solidarity. I have tried to realize Albright in the texts of myth and social processes, inscribed as it were outside the flesh. I believe that describing such linguistic-social dynamics offers one way, with a postmodern tilt, to speak of sociological "reality."

Third, theory and practice imply an altered notion of biblical studies as an academic discipline. You recall that I spoke earlier (page 9) of discursive practice as systematic uses of language according to consensually approved, discipline-specific codes that form the "object" of which they speak. Consider the "Bible" in biblical studies. From this point of view, postmodernist discourse decenters the privileged scientific-rational or modernist codes that frame a "Bible-out-there" as inert object to be understood and mastered.[5] Multiple Bibles emerge in the dynamics of contested social processes— devotion, worship, hermeneutics, historical explanation, philological study.

---

5. One might construct an interesting history of biblical interpretation by exploring how traditional devotional and theological focus on the Bible-out-there fell together with Enlightenment rationalism, allies as it were, in creating space for a certain kind of modernist religiosity.

In this view, the mix of perspectives forms the linguistic-social substance of our academic discipline, rather than a *single*, stable text awaiting proper understanding by trained exegetes.

I do not imagine the shift in viewpoint victoriously, as though one view supplants, buries another. I rather think of alternative, in some ways intersecting, realities made of a Bible given us. Thus, histories of our academic discipline formed in postmodern discourse would be constructed with due attention to perspectivity of knowledge. They would not focus, as in a modernist mode, on Master Knowers who advanced objective knowledge about that enigmatic but stable text-out-there grasped by applying privileged discourse and sensibilities.

Well, you can see, John, I think the theoretical perspective I have adopted makes more than a little difference to the ways of proceeding. The shift surely need not mean the end of cooperative ventures, or conversations across paradigmatic divides. The essays I have written are intended (what a modernist thought—an author's intentionality!) to suggest steps toward figuring out what we biblical critics do, and do differently. Here I may claim the power of difference in situations of knowledge-making where will to define center, and therefore margin *from* the center, is frequently encountered and to be resisted in the name of honoring difference. This strain of tolerant liberality, a part of postmodern embrace of pluralism that has its taproot in aspects of the European Enlightenment, suggests once again those permeable borders of modernism-postmodernism transformations that are a part of our future.

Select Bibliography

I. Archival Sources

Albright, William Foxwell. Papers. American Philosophical Society, Philadelphia.
Biblical Colloquium. Records. In possession of Edward F. Campbell, Jr., McCormick Theological Seminary, Chicago.
Freedman, David Noel. Correspondence. In possession of Freedman, University of California, San Diego.
Morgenstern, Julian. Papers. American Jewish Archives, Cincinnati.

II. Bibliographical Resources

Beck, Astrid, et al. *Fortunate the Eyes That See: Essays in Honor of David Noel Freedman*. Grand Rapids: William B. Eerdmans Publishing Co., 1995.
Cross, Frank Moore, Jr., et al. *Magnalia Dei. The Mighty Acts of God: Essays on the Bible and Archaeology in Memory of G. Ernest Wright*. Garden City, N.Y.: Doubleday, 1976.
Freedman, David Noel. *The Published Works of William Foxwell Albright: A Comprehensive Bibliography*. Cambridge, Mass.: American Schools of Oriental Research, 1975.
Huffmon, Herbert, et al. *The Quest for the Kingdom of God: Studies in Honor of George E. Mendenhall*. Winona Lake, Ind.: Eisenbrauns, 1983.
Levine, Baruch, and Abraham Malamat, eds. *Harry Orlinsky Volume. Eretz-Israel* 16 (1982). Jerusalem: Israel Exploration Society.
Mays, James, ed. "The History of Israel and Biblical Faith: In Honor of John Bright." *Interpretation* 29, no. 2 (1975).
Meyers, Carol, and M. O'Connor. *The Word Shall Go Forth: Essays in Honor of David Noel Freedman*. Winona Lake, Ind.: Eisenbrauns, 1983.
Miller, Patrick, et al. *Ancient Israelite Religion: Essays in Honor of Frank Moore Cross*. Philadelphia: Fortress Press, 1987.

Orlinsky, Harry. *An Indexed Bibliography of the Writings of William Foxwell Albright.* New Haven: American Schools of Oriental Research, 1941.

III. Assessments of Albright and the Albrighteans

Campbell, Edward F., and J. Maxwell Miller. "W. F. Albright and Historical Reconstruction [with reply by J. M. Miller]." *Biblical Archaeologist* 42 (December 1979): 37–47.

Cross, Frank M., Jr. "W. F. Albright's View of Biblical Archaeology and Its Methodology." *Biblical Archaeologist* 36 (February 1973): 2–5.

Cross, Frank M., Jr., et al. "George Ernest Wright in Memoriam." *Newsletter of the American Schools of Oriental Research*, no. 3 (September 1974): 1–8.

Dever, William G. *Recent Archaeological Discoveries and Biblical Research.* Seattle: University of Washington Press, 1990.

Feigen, Samuel I. "Professor William Foxwell Albright." *Bitzaron* (February 1947): 303–13. [Hebrew]

Freedman, David Noel. "In Memoriam G. E. Wright." *Bulletin of the American Schools of Oriental Research* 220 (December 1975): 3.

———. *The Published Works of William Foxwell Albright: A Comprehensive Bibliography.* Cambridge, Mass.: American Schools of Oriental Research, 1975: 3–40.

Hardwick, S. E. *Change and Constancy in William Foxwell Albright's Treatment of Early Old Testament History and Religion, 1918–1958.* Ann Arbor, Mich.: University Microfilms, 1965.

Hopkins, David, ed. "Celebrating and Examining W. F. Albright." *Biblical Archaeologist* 56, no. 1 (March 1993): 3–45.

Horn, Siegfried H. "The Book Albright Never Finished: All Efforts at Publication Now Ended [The History of the Religion of Israel]." *Biblical Archaeology Review* 10, no. 1 (January 1984): 64–68.

King, Philip J. *American Archaeology in the Mideast: A History of the American Schools of Oriental Research.* Philadelphia: American Schools of Oriental Research, 1983.

———. "The Influence of G. Ernest Wright on the Archaeology of Palestine." In *Archaeology and Biblical Interpretation: Essays in Memory of Dr. Glenn Rose*, edited by Leo Perdue et al., 15–29. Atlanta: John Knox Press, 1987.

Long, Burke O. "Historical Imaginings, Ideological Gestures: W. F. Albright and the 'Reasoning Faculties of Man.'" In *The Archaeology of Israel: Constructing the Past/Interpreting the Present*, edited by Neil Silberman. Sheffield, England: Sheffield Academic Press [forthcoming].

———. "W. F. Albright as Prophet-Reformer: A Theological Paradigm Inscribed in Scholarly Practice." In *Prophets and Paradigms: Essays in Honor of Gene M. Tucker*, edited by Stephen B. Reid. Sheffield, England. Sheffield Academic Press [forthcoming].

Mendenhall, George E. "Biblical Interpretation and the Albright School." In *Archaeology and Biblical Interpretation: Essays in Memory of Dr. Glenn Rose*, edited by Leo Perdue et al., 3–13. Atlanta: John Knox Press, 1987.

Miles, John A. "Understanding Albright: A Revolutionary Étude." *Harvard Theo-
    logical Review* 69 (January 1976): 151–75.
Moorey, P. R. *A Century of Biblical Archaeology*. Cambridge: Lutterworth, 1991.
Running, Leona Glidden, and David Noel Freedman. *William Foxwell Albright: A
    Twentieth-Century Genius*. New York: Morgan Press, 1975.
Van Beek, Gus W., ed., *The Scholarship of William Foxwell Albright: An Appraisal*.
    Harvard Semitic Studies 33. Atlanta: Scholars Press, 1989.

Index